DATE DUE

JY 30 98			
DE			

DOWNSCALING

DOWNSCALING

DOWNSCALING

DOWNSCALING

DOWNSCALING

*Simplify and Enrich
Your Lifestyle*

Dave and Kathy Babbit

MOODY PRESS

CHICAGO

ISBN: 0-8024-1784-1

1 3 5 7 9 10 8 6 4 2

Printed in the United States of America

It is to our three children,
Jeannette, Kimberly, and Dione,
that we dedicate this work,
for they are the reason we have
chosen to downscale our lifestyle

Contents

Authors' Note

This book is not meant to be a financial, psychological, medical, or theological work. Should questions arise in those areas, please consult with a professional in the respective field. Stories are usually true, but may be a compilation to protect identities or to fit the need of the illustration.

Acknowledgments

We would like to thank all those wonderful people who have shared their stories with us. We especially appreciate Al and Raeann Hart of Hart and Hart Advertising, Warsaw, Indiana, for their help in launching our newsletter, *Downscaling 46510*.

Families
for Sale

PART 1

1

Rekindling the Original Dream

Downscaling. Russ knows what it is.

As a young man he studied for the priesthood. He completed several undergraduate degrees and took considerable work toward a graduate degree. Then he decided to reconsider his options and try a variety of jobs. When he was twenty-eight, a friend found him a low-paying job right at the bottom of a company—but a job that had possibilities. Russ took it. He intended to remain a bachelor, make lots of money, and live in the fast lane.

The first year he made $13,000. By the end of his sixth year with the company he was making $53,000 a year plus bonuses. Two years after joining the company, Russ departed from his original intention and got married. But he insisted that he be the sole worker in the house. Russ and his wife lived out the typical American dream. They bought a house and a new car, and they had children.

When Russ was thirty-four he was offered a management position, complete with a large cash bonus if he accepted. For the next six years, he managed the most productive territory of his company. He worked twelve to fifteen hours a day. He had completely bought into the American dream of success—which only bred in him the desire for more success and more money. He shut everything out of his life except his job. By this time, he owned a Mercedes-Benz and a myriad of other toys.

Then Russ's attitude began to change.

His wife was becoming more and more alienated from him. She was lonely, living her own life and raising the children by herself. Gradually success wore thin on Russ, too, and his early seminary training began to gnaw at his conscience. Relationships were becoming more important, whereas the glory of work was fading.

In 1990 things came to a head. That year Russ earned almost $20,000 in bonuses. But because the company wouldn't show profitability if it actually paid the bonuses, Russ and others like him never received the money they had worked so hard for. Russ couldn't help thinking, *Here I am. I have given so much of myself to this company, and now they do this to me!*

Hurt and anger caused him to consider more deeply what he was doing with his life. He had gotten to the point where a lifestyle of conspicuous consumption had become a trap. He knew he had to get out of it. He went to his superior at the company and explained that he didn't want to be in management any longer. Instead, he wanted an outside sales position with less responsibility. So the company gave him a one-year severance payment from his managerial position at his current salary of $92,000 and a new job: turn around an unproductive sales territory.

Today Russ and his wife are using the severance pay to pay off their debts. They have one car payment, no credit card balance, rarely eat out, and live on a budget. They no longer throw money away on designer clothes. They shop at sales, and Russ's wife has begun to sew more of their clothes. Gone are the thirty dollar style cuts; in are eight dollar haircuts. Russ discontinued the lawn service and now does his own. He got rid of the Mercedes-Benz and bought a Honda. He is planning to pay off the house debt with stock options.

Russ is now the regular host at the family's evening meal, and he has time to take his kids to school. He and his wife are cultivating their relationship—something that was neglected during his period of career advancement. They experience much less personal stress, and Russ has the time to become involved in more meaningful activities with his family through his church and community.

DEFINING DOWNSCALING

Russ is not alone in feeling that there has to be a better way to live than that symbolized by the typical American success story.

Many Americans are finding that a lifestyle of consumption is not worth the cost. They dread the maze of meaningless commitments, suffocating memories, and unfulfilled dreams that sums up their existence. They can no longer stand to be bogged down with clutter in their homes and in their lives that forces them to function in a continual state of stress. Many have even opted for apathy in order to deaden the overwhelming sense of confusion and pain of unrealistic demands and unmet expectations.

Castles appear beautiful and stately on the outside. But in reality, they have no central heating and originally had no indoor plumbing. Cold drafts and damp, musty odors permeate their massive rooms. We have visited several European castles, with their infamous dungeons and ornate trappings. Many castles are for sale. Many are in various states of disrepair and the owners lack the cash flow for necessary maintenance. Those who have inherited the monstrosities are finding that the upkeep is not worth the steep cost.

Twentieth-century living in America lends itself to a lifestyle that is painless in its inception but deadly in its fruition. We have become a people encumbered by unnecessary weights threatening to strangle even those rare occasions of happiness. Many of us are fed up with trying to have it all. We have accumulated a warehouse of things and lost our families in the process. The masquerade of the pursuit of money, power, and prestige is being stripped of its facade, revealing emptiness and frustration. The quest for materialism has diminished the average family's closeness, values, and sense of satisfaction. More and more Americans are deciding that this frenzied existence isn't worth the sacrifices made on behalf of a fruitless dream.

We sometimes wish life would ease up, but we fear that if we try to take even a short breather, we will get stomped in the process. All too often, we get stomped anyway—broken relationships born of the strain of constant neglect, damaged health begotten through adulterated lifestyles, insecurity springing from unkept promises, and crushed spirits battered by insensitive slanderers all set the stage for slow self-destruction.

In our struggle to meet the expectations of others, and perhaps even our own, many of us come face-to-face with emptiness, frustration, distrust of others, and loneliness. We live in a constant state of worry, always trying to "see how we are doing" in comparison to others. We latch on to fame, power, or possessions to try to end our inner dissatisfaction.

Doubt and bitterness enter our self-made prisons. We have the sense of having lived in vain, of not being free to explore life with all of its adventures and possibilities.

As a result, an undercurrent called "downscaling" is sweeping the nation, coaxing families back to the old-fashioned dinner hour with dads as Cub Scout leaders, moms hosting little girls' sleepovers, and kids feeling the difference. Recent surveys document the shift of Americans toward a more relaxed life. Many are opting for a lifestyle that allows time for personal needs, families, and friends —concerns nudged out during the success craze of the '80s when people became so caught up in titles, job descriptions, and salaries that they lost their true identities and work become the thermometer of self-worth.[1]

Time magazine calls the movement back to home life and basic values "pervasive" and says it is evident at all levels of society.[2] *USA Today* dubbed downscaling the "trend of the decade."[3] A *Fortune* magazine poll of working Americans in their twenties found that instead of riches, 75 percent are "more concerned with a rich family or spiritual life, a rewarding job, the chance to help others, and the opportunity for leisure and travel or for intellectual and creative enrichment."[4]

Downscaling involves making changes to bring balance back into your life. In a newsletter we publish about downscaling, David wrote:

> Downscaling is about margins and limits. We abuse financial limits by living beyond our income. We abuse physical limits by not getting adequate rest nor eating properly. We abuse our emotional limits by subjecting ourselves to more and more stress.
>
> Our society has helped us by providing a set of peripheral industries to deal with stress, time management, financial planning, and debt consolidation. Instead of setting rational limits, we hire services to help us continually live beyond them.[5]

Downscaling is asking yourself, "How much income can we live on comfortably but not excessively?" It is understanding that hunger for money loses its addictive power when we are satisfied and fulfilled in other areas of our lives. It is realizing that success is not measured in tangibles, but is a process of investing in the intangibles of daily living.

When the Oakland fire and Hurricane Andrew ravaged any normalcy its victims may have had, what remained were charred and battered ruins of "the good life." Relationships were all that was left, relationships that had already been devastated by a more insidious tragedy than a hurricane or fire—insidious because it wreaked its devastation by quiet, cumulative effect; a tragedy because marriages and families were broken and destroyed by unwise choices. How many of us will regret the choices we are making even today?

ASSESSING THE DREAM

Russ had to come to the point where he needed to evaluate his lifestyle, circumstances, and desires. He needed to ask himself what the end result would be if he continued the pattern he had set for himself. Each of us would benefit from doing the same. We are responsible, not for what others do, but for how we live. To help you determine the specific needs and desires that are unique to you, take this "Personal Needs Assessment" quiz.

1. On a sheet of paper list three to five emotional needs that are important to you and why.

Examples: I need to love and be loved. (It's foundational.)
I need challenges. (They motivate me.)
I need some independence. (It gives me a sense of control.)
I need to be spontaneous. (It makes life more fun.)
I need solitude. (It gives me a sense of well-being.)

2. Name several physical needs that when filled seem to make you happy and why.
Examples: I need to enjoy nature. (It offers a sense of peacefulness.)
I need adventure. (It adds zest to life.)
I need the physical relationship with my spouse. (It's enjoyable and draws us closer.)
I need to be physically fit. (It makes me feel good.)
I need variety in my work. (It keeps me interested.)

3. What mental needs have you been ignoring that are important to you? Why are you happier when they are met?
Examples: I need to be organized. (It helps my life go smoother.)
I need to be creative and dream. (It adds enrichment to my life.)
I need to use and stimulate my mind. (It stretches me.)

4. What about needs in other categories (spiritual, nature, creativity, giving, and so on)? Name a few and think about why they are important to you.
Examples: I need to teach. (It's my contribution to humanity.)
I need a relationship with God. (It gives meaning to life.)
I need to write and paint. (They are extensions of myself.)
I need to positively influence others. (It gives me joy.)[6]

Much of living involves taking risks. We will miss many opportunities for growing, learning, and experiencing—some enjoyable, some not so enjoyable—if we become complacent, lazy, and comfortable. Often we are afraid to step out of our comfort zones. We would rather suffer with the familiar than have to deal with change or a new circumstance. We limit ourselves and settle for living mediocre lives rather than participating in the rich splendor of all that life has to offer.

One fear we have is that we won't measure up to a standard of perfection set by society, our parents, or ourselves. Understanding and dealing with our limitations is part of the process of maturing. Did you ever have a vacuum cleaner demonstration in your home? Kathy is a very good housekeeper. But when the salesman showed her the dust and dirt her own vacuum had missed, she felt a sense of despair. It was the same feeling she gets when she goes to the hairdresser and the stylist suggests this treatment or that conditioner to improve the manageability or bounce of her hair. Or the feeling she gets when she visits the dentist and hears that this cosmetic procedure or that filling replacement will perfect the flaws in her teeth. It's a sinking feeling of not measuring up in some way, of falling below the line of perfection. But the reality is, life will never be perfect, nor any part of it. We only cause ourselves undue frustration by trying to live up to perfection. We only decrease our enjoyment of life by being afraid to try something new for fear of failing to reach an unobtainable illusion.

ADDING REALITY TO YOUR DREAM

After you have worked through the "Personal Needs Assessment" quiz, go over the plan again. Begin to eliminate things from your life that don't line up with the direction you would really like to go—that extra committee you felt you should be on to please your cousin; the Saturday morning golf game to garner business contacts when you hate golf; the overtime you put in, not out of necessity, but because you are addicted to your work and have a low self-image. Then make the appropriate changes. If someday you would like to own a floral shop, read books about owning a business and take some training in floral design. Establish a savings account for start-up costs. Take steps to actually accomplish what you really desire instead of just thinking about it. Any progress you make will be more beneficial than doing nothing.

If you try something and it doesn't work, try a different approach. Sometimes we only find out what is right for us by first trying something that is not suited to us. Kathy has tried lots of things over the years, some of which have included owning a small craft company, teaching children writing skills, playing the piano, sewing, gardening, cake decorating, various sporting activities, running political campaigns, and doing fund-raising. At the respective times in her life, each of these was fun, provided a valuable learning experience, and offered a sense of fulfillment. But the common denominator she found was that though each was interesting, none was right for her to pursue on a long-term basis. Still, she has lived a richer life for having tried, and she has became more convinced of the areas better suited for her.

We need to make time to enjoy what we do. As fast-paced Americans, we have trained ourselves to jump from one accomplishment to the next without really standing back and appreciating the process. It's like cleaning a closet. The goal is an organized closet with the trash, nonessentials, and overflow removed. After we have invested time and energy cleaning the closet, we have a tendency to rush to the next project. How rewarding it would be if we first stopped to appreciate our efforts—the order we have brought to disorder and the beauty of our creativity in the way we arranged, eliminated, and organized.

What about the last time you washed your car—cleaned it inside and out until it sparkled? Did you take a moment and breathe in a sense of satisfaction for a job well-done? Or did you hurriedly rush to the next item on your "to do" list?

If taking the time to appreciate our work is important, how much more valuable it is to take the time to appreciate the people closest to us. When was the last time you stopped long enough to tell someone thank you or complimented your spouse for doing a routine chore that you have taken for granted? When have you encouraged your kids to "keep up the good work"?

Over the years, for a variety of reasons (usually the cost or lack of equipment) our family has failed to take photographs of our numerous experiences. We have seen and done more unusual things than the average person will do in several lifetimes. How valuable those photographs would be today to us and our children if we had only taken them. As we grow older, we more fully appreciate what they could have meant to us. At the time, it seemed as though the kids would always be young or our experiences in Africa or Europe would be hard to forget. But as our memories have dimmed over the years, we have come to see that an effort and slight expense back then would be paying rich dividends today.

So, too, do we sometimes come to the close of our lives regretting lost moments and opportunities for making memories with our children or spouse. How easy it is to assume they will always be there. How comfortable we have become in just drifting from day to day without making the effort to create lasting experiences with those most important to us. Spend your life investing in people, not in regrets, and you will rekindle the original dream of enjoying meaningful relationships and living a full life.

NOTES

1. Donna Jackson, "Making a Choice," *New Woman,* April 1992, 69.
2. Janice Castro, "The Simple Life," *Time,* 8 April 1991, 59.
3. Joe Urschel, "Depression Chic? Making a Virtue of Necessity," *USA Today,* 28 April 1992, editorial page.
4. Alan Deutschman, "The Upbeat Generation," *Fortune,* 13 July 1992, 42.
5. David Babbitt, "Letter from the Publisher," *Downscaling 46510,* June 1992, 2.
6. Kathy Babbitt, "Your 'Personal Needs Assessment,'" *Downscaling 46510,* July 1992, 1, 8.

2

Good-bye to Brown Bag Lunches, Used Cars, and Rented Cottages

Why do Americans put up with a frenetic pace of life, and is it worth it? Peggy knows why she did it, and she also knows that it isn't worth it.

She began the slide into a frustrating lifestyle by starting a business to help with the family income. At first things seemed positive. Her cottage industry grew from $600 to what would have been $40,000 a year if she had kept at it. In four years she had doubled her family's income. But there was a cost. "I thought at the time I was trapped doing the job forever, because for the first time we could afford the things we always dreamed of having. But we had gotten to the point of consumption as entertainment. While buying things became less of a problem, finding time to do the special things that had become my 'trademark' seemed impossible. I worked from 6:00 A.M. to 6:00 P.M. five days a week, fifty weeks a year.

"Two years ago, I was frustrated and depressed because the things that had been left behind were all my crafts—all the 'how tos' that had my name on them. My house was falling apart, and I just didn't have any time to put it together. I felt like Humpty Dumpty. Day melted into night. One day became another without my knowing it. I couldn't keep track of time."[1]

Peggy's motive for starting her business was a worthy one—helping her family—but sometimes people accept a hurried family life for more selfish reasons. They have taken too seriously the saying, "Fake it till you make it." So intent are they on playing the part of success that they allow bank credit to perpetuate the illusion. When that is coupled with permitting an employer to play the role of God, it isn't long before these people lose their identities in order to become a clone of the "image." They believe that the only true means of success is through ascending the corporate ladder. This mind-set is partly what prompted Americans to work almost 160 hours more a year in 1989 than they did in 1969.[2]

Underscoring the need to maintain a facade of success is the desire to feel needed within the hierarchy of the corporation. This desire stems from a basic human characteristic and isn't necessarily unhealthy. The problem is that the need cannot truly be met simply through devotion to an employer. The result is frustration, emptiness, and dissatisfaction.

Another motivation behind the success syndrome is the desire for control. We believe that we can control our destinies by controlling our little worlds. Some of us go to great lengths to achieve that sense of control. We nag, connive, deceive, threaten, maneuver, manipulate, and rationalize, all the while convincing ourselves it is for the good of those involved. Yet, whether we seek control of others, circumstances, or our future, the quest for control is often useless and frustrating.

Some of us box ourselves into a stress-filled life by allowing others to control us. We are bombarded by pressures from family members, society, and ourselves to embrace an unrealistic perspective on getting ahead. As the pressures increase, some make ethical compromises that are the first steps in a slow desensitization process that will eventually destroy their personhood. Outwitting the competition, working as a team to make the company number one, giving up everything for the sake of an unfeeling corporation—these are the tenets so many have willingly bought into. Too late they realize that it was all a lie. When it is all over, they are like slaves left for dead, having spent their souls foolishly.

When a couple first marries, they think they can survive on love. But as they sink into the mire of wanting more and more, the love they had for one another originally is choked off. Career ascension overtakes a couple's time, energies, and passions. Materialism draws them away from their pledge to love "'til death us do part." Life becomes a treadmill of going to work, making money to pay the bills, arguing about the children, running from one activity to the next, all the while becoming more and more unsatisfied.

As two-career families become the norm, a competitive spirit develops in many marriage. A team spirit of pulling together to nurture the family unit is replaced by selfishness and independence. One tragic consequence of this trend can be seen in divorce statistics. As of late 1990, there were 9.3 million single parents in this country, many of whom are dependent upon others for child-care. Live-in nannies, day-care centers, schools, friends, relatives, sitters, and neighbors make up the framework of their daily existence.[3] When it comes to the children, the value system promoted by today's media leaves permanent scars.

Along with the quest for the affluent life comes the tendency to give our kids too much—too much money to spend without responsibility, too much freedom without limits, too much pressure to become "somebody," too much food, and too many activities. With the overload come physical, emotional, and psychological problems rarely found in the kids of generations past.[4]

Then there is relocation trauma. When a move is made for selfish reasons and not for the family's best interest, anger and resentment often take hold. Even when a move is made for the good of the family, there is always a period of adjusting. Adjusting to new schools, neighborhoods, friends, activities, and schedules causes anxiety to many a family member. True, a move may result in opportunities for growth and challenge and unique experiences, but sometimes one more move can be one too many.

In our own series of relocations, we came to the point where we hoped each move would be our last. After a particularly difficult move, when the empty boxes had been hauled away, the cupboards organized throughout the house, and the kids settled in a new school, Kathy breathed a sigh of resignation. Many of our moves had offered new challenges she eagerly anticipated. Experiencing different cultures throughout the world and enjoying a cross-section of society in the United States usually excited her. Even though we exchanged good-byes through tears, she was always ready to make new friends in the next community.

But this last move had a deeper emotional impact on her than had the earlier ones. As we drove to our new home, each mile imprinted on her heart the reality of severed bonds. We had left close

friends we wished could have come with us. Kathy knew that the relationships we had developed would change once we weren't near our friends. She was right. Long letters helped to alleviate the pain of missing our friends. Phone calls helped to soothe the ache for their presence. Yet over the months the dynamics of her friendships changed in subtle ways. No longer would Kathy's best friend call to relate important news or share the struggles of her life. Letters would offer less and less depth and take on a more superficial tone. It took six months of reclusive living before Kathy could reenter the mainstream of life in a new community and again become comfortable with reaching out. If the move was hard for her as an adult, how much more difficult it must have been for our children.[5]

Travel is another drawback of modern employment. An increasing amount of business travel is necessary for an employee to advance in his profession and for his company to keep pace with the current level of productivity. According to the U.S. Travel Data Center, 5 million business travelers in 1990 took ten or more trips a year.[6] Constantly forced to choose between family needs and employment concerns, the frequent business traveler often thinks about changing jobs. But fear of loss of income keeps many from actually taking steps in that direction. So they continue in their overstressed lifestyle, become even more emotionally and physically depleted, and lose family closeness in the process.

She was a high school student. Now, after six months of hospitalization she was coming home. Would the kids at school accept her? Would she be able to overcome the stigma of having gone through "treatment"?

The months away had had been traumatic, stretching, and painful, but she was finally declared "healthy." Yet nagging doubts caused her unrest. She had been told that many of her problems stemmed from a weak relationship with her father. He seemed never to be home, always working hard to "provide for the family." Even when he was home, he was emotionally distant, unwilling to invest himself in her life.

She had gravitated toward guys to fill the emptiness. She never lacked for dates or attention, but she wondered if that popularity was because of who she was as a person or only because she was attractive and filled a need in her dates' lives.

She used to dream about sitting on her daddy's lap and having him read her a story. How she wished he had been the one to help her learn to ride a two-wheeler. How she longed to hear her father shouting her name at one of her volleyball games.

It hurt not to hear him affirm her the day she was to take her driver's test. At school, girls would tell about "dates" with their dads and what fun they had together. She could only pretend in daydreams. When her friends' fathers sent them flowers for special occasions, her heart ached for all the roses she never received.

Would it have been different had her father played his rightful role? Her counselors thought so. But now—would he be any different? Would he be there for her when she needed him more than ever. How she yeared to hold her father's hand for the rest of the journey.

A father's absence, either physical or emotional, can have severe consequences for his children. When we bought our lakefront property, a stately maple tree graced the front lawn and overshadowed our dock. A few months after we moved in, a fall thunderstorm took its toll on the maple. One of the largest branches cracked and fell with a crash. A sickening feeling came over us as we witnessed the partial loss of springtime splendor, summertime shade, fall artistry, and winter magic. Our tree looked strong and healthy, magnificent and solid. But it was hollow at the core, rotten and weak. So when the winds blew, the branch gave way and was ripped from the trunk.

Today's families, like that maple, may seem strong and secure, but at the core many are weak and deteriorating. The family has become a shell of the original dream and has ceased to the be the lifeblood of the community. Family members bicker and tear one another down. The result is physical and emotional poverty. The poverty rate among single-parent families is 33.4 percent as compared to 5.7 percent among two-parent families.[7] Only sixteen percent of divorced parents are custodial fathers.[8] Broken families produce more than 80 percent of the adolescents in psychiatric hospitals.[9] Again, the children bear the brunt of our selfishness.

Larry Poland says that raising "a fatherless child in America today, white or black, male or female, increases something like tenfold the chance of that child ending up a permanent member of an impoverished underclass. Even ignoring economics, a whopping disproportion of boys who grow up in fatherless homes commit rape, homicide, suicide, assault; succumb to drug addiction, mental illness, get low grades or drop out of school, and engage in all kinds of crime and delinquency."[10] Moreover, "father-absent households" are not just those where no father is present. They include households where the father is physically present but emotionally absent.

Today there is a cultural shift from even raising children at all. According to the Census Bureau, childless families today outnumber those with children.[11] Couples are opting not to have children in favor of a more carefree lifestyle. Two-career couples now number almost sixty percent of all households.[12] Children are a burden, are expensive, and involve taking risks. For the first time in several decades, the number of people deciding that the cost is too high is greater than the number who elect to make the investment.

Even for those who make the investment in children, "dual-income families enjoy just marginal monetary advantages over families in which only the husband works."[13] That work often takes its toll on family life. "In the mid-'80's," Drew says,

> after several years of [managing a branch office of my company], I began to realize my daily routine was solving every one else's problems. I had no time to solve my own, if I even knew what they were. I was working long, hard hours and driving two and one-half hours a day round-trip to

work. What was all this for? A large six-figure income. The privilege of being a branch manager and going to all the boring meetings. Having shoulder and chest pains most of the time. Worrying about when my ulcers would start up again and when I would have time for my next meal. And, worst of all, not having the time to spend with my family.[14]

In the struggle to reach an often elusive dream, a pattern develops in the quest for success. First comes an inner longing to be someone of importance. In believing the myths hailed by the world, we set our course. Misplaced goals and priorities maneuver us through a maze of choices. Then with unwise decisions comes entrapment to a system that erodes our deepest sense of fulfillment. In the vacuum, we one day recognize that all we have to show for our life of dedication to the myth is unhappiness. And then it hits us—we finally understand that the happiest days of our lives were the ones marked by brown bag lunches, rented castles, and used cars. We have chased empty rainbows only to discover a pot of fool's gold.

NOTES

1. "Letter of the Month," *Downscaling 46510,* June 1992, 3.
2. David P. Willis, "U.S. Workers: More Hours, 'Stressed Out,'" *USA Today,* 18 February 1992, 1A.
3. Philip Elmer-DeWitt, "The Great Experiment," *Time,* Special Issue, Fall 1990, 73.
4. Ralph E. Minear and William Proctor, *Kids Who Have Too Much* (Nashville: Thomas Nelson, 1989).
5. Kathy J. Babbitt, "One More Time," *Aglow,* January/February 1991, 24.
6. Desiree French, "On the Road: Families Pay the Toll," *USA Today,* 30 October 1991, 2E.
7. James Dobson, monthly newsletter, June 1992, 2.
8. Penelope Wang and Elizabeth Fenner, "How You Can Live Your American Dream," *Money,* November 1992, 168.
9. Joe Klein, "Whose Values?" *Newsweek,* 8 June 1992, 21.
10. Larry W. Poland, "Prayer Focus," *Mediator* 7, no. 3 (1992), 2.
11. Andrea Stone, "Family 'Shift': Most Households Have No Children," *USA Today,* 8 May 1992, 10A.
12. Wang and Fenner, 173.
13. Bob Jones, "The Mommy Market," *Entrepreneur* 20, no. 9 (September 1992), 62.
14. "Letter of the Month," *Downscaling 46510,* August 1992, 6.

3

Rainbow Chasers

We were both doing volunteer work in Alaska the summer we met. Actually, for Dave the volunteer work was a continuation of what he had begun the summer before. He had stayed through the winter instead of returning to his home state of Michigan. During that year in Alaska he had spent several months living with a bush pilot. It was then that he decided to follow a similar career. Kathy was in Alaska on a special program sponsored by the college she was attending.

The unique setting led to a quick romance. Seeing each other day in, day out allowed us to view one another in all types of situations. On this particular day, Dave was nervous and not his usual easy-going self. Finally he choked out, "I have fourteen dollars in my pocket and I never expect to be rich. I want to be a jungle pilot, and the pay won't be very good. But I love you, and want to spend the rest of my life with you. Would you marry me?" So began the dream. With little desire to acquire material wealth, we set out to reach the goal of living and working overseas.

SCRAPPING THE ORIGINAL BLUEPRINT

After eleven years of training, preparation, and language school, we were on our way. However, our plans diverged from our original blueprint because of a choice we made regarding our responsibility as parents. During the three years we spent in Africa, our children needed to be sent away to school for three months at a time. Their school bus was either a small aircraft or an open truck over roads that gave new meaning to the word.

Each parting was a bittersweet occasion. For us as parents it was a time of letting go, a season of sadness as the house assumed a strange quietness. Gone were the rooms ringing with shouts of laughter and childish interchanges. No longer were our identities as parents affirmed on a daily basis. The yearning for the end of the three-month term began even in the first hours of separation.

For the children parting was a time of excitement and a season of opportunities and giddy reunions with schoolmates from faraway outstations. Although the children at the school—some as young as first grade—experienced the frightening agony of separation, it was made more bearable by the anticipation of new adventures and friendships. Independence and maturity came to these children earlier than to their peers stateside. A worldview rarely embraced by those so young began to take hold and shape their personalities and minds.

In spite of the positives of sending our children away to boarding school, the weight of our responsibility as parents was the foundation of our decision to return to the States. Kathy remembers the first time she went to visit Kimberly midway through her first term of first grade. Kathy was in Kim's dorm room with some other children. Kim walked right by her mother, not a flicker of recognition on her face. Our daughter was growing up not even knowing who we were, nor us understanding who she was. The long separations were not conducive to our family's developing the relationships that were of prime importance to us.

FOREIGNERS AT HOME

Upon our return to the States, we spent a year in the home office, where Dave served manager of recruitment for our organization. During that time we evaluated our direction for the future, and that was important in helping us to decide what we should do next. But what affected us the most is what some call "reverse culture shock." We all had adjustments to make. One daughter wanted to know where we could make a fire to boil water to drink and for a hot bath. Another asked if it was safe to go barefoot, or would we get jiggers in our toes? And the third talked about how strange the walls looked without lizards crawling all over them.

Reverse culture shock hit Kathy on her first trip to the grocery store. The store was just as foreign to her as the culture we had recently left. Here were rows of cereals to choose from. In Africa we often had only hot cereal cooked from wheat berries, or occasionally one or two kinds of boxed cereal. Here were many different variations of catsup and salad dressing. On the mission station we made all our own from scratch. Here were foods in boxes and jars and cans that we had never even seen before. Kathy left the store with only a few purchases, unable to assimilate so much mental confusion at one time.

Dave's response to our reentry into American culture came in the form of a rejection of materialism. After seeing poverty daily just outside our door for three years, the unappreciated wealth of the average American created turmoil in him that took time to resolve. Dave reshaped his view of our responsibility even when we live in a land of plenty. We would avoid conspicuous consumption and focus on developing relationships and accomplishing that which was permanent and not temporary.

IN THE STATES BUT NOT TOGETHER

Our determination to live simply did not get put into practice immediately. At first, in fact, we were diverted from it. Upon deciding not to return to Africa so that we could remain intact as a family, we moved to Alaska, where Dave had taken a flying job. Thus began the trap of pursuing bigger and better equipment in order to secure a higher salary. Yet we never seemed to be doing anything other than holding up the status quo in our acquisition of things. Dave's salary was eaten up by taxes, private school tuition, and living expenses.

Over the years our mind-set changed from a determination to avoid conspicuous consumption to an acceptance of its demise in our lives as middle-class Americans. We were not steeped in consumerism, but we did allow Dave's career path to limit our growth and closeness as a family. In Africa, when Dave was flying small aircraft on jungle routes he sometimes felt an undercurrent of regret, thinking that he was missing out by not flying bigger equipment and being part of the fast track in aviation. Now he realizes that he wasn't missing anything when weighed against the backdrop of negataives that accompany the fast track.

He came to that view the hard way. Because the aviation industry is so fickle, moves are common for pilots and their families. In addition to the moves we made during a stint in the navy and the years of preparation for overseas service, we moved forty-four times in less than twenty-two years of marriage. During a two-year period, Dave was gone from home more than 480 days. He had become the classic absentee father. He was losing touch with what was most important to him—his family.

Although the girls gained valuable worldwide experience, a certain amount of insecurity and rootlessness left its mark on the children's lives. They became hesitant to develop friendships because it hurt too much to leave friends behind time after time. A feeling of restlessness underscored their relationships. The temporary had overtaken that which is permanent.

BACK TO THE COUNTRYSIDE

During his long days away from home Dave felt his frustration mounting and realized that even if he had to leave aviation behind, he needed to make a drastic change. Flying was challenging and enjoyable—and his livelihood—but if he was to gain time with his family, he had to be willing to give it up.

While Dave was still on a contract, with one month home and one month away, we poured over maps of various states, researched statistics regarding cost-of-living indexes, and read information on the benefits of living in different parts of the country. We even took a week-long house-hunting trip to the Lake Tahoe area. After landing in Reno, we rented a car and drove some two thousand miles to check out a three-state area. Although the region was beautiful, the cost-of-living and taxes were not. We looked at $100,000 shanties and thought that for the area the price was good. How warped our sense of value had become in less than a week.

Then, during the summer a year ago, Dave was in Paris, Kathy house-sitting in Florida, and our oldest daughter taking care of children in San Francisco. Within a twenty-four hour period we all came up with the idea of moving back to an area where we had lived for a year fourteen years earlier during our preparation for going overseas—and this was without our having mentioned this particular area previously, although we were in the process of making the choice for a "permanent" move.

We knew the cost of living was one of the lowest in the nation. It had distinct seasons, something we had missed during our four-year stay in Texas, and we still had friends in the area. So we loaded up a rental trailer and made the move to our current location in the Midwest.

Dave had always wanted to live on a lake, so our first day in town entailed a lake- and house-hunting expedition. Before meeting the realtor, Dave cautioned Kathy to remain calm and not express interest in any property. The plan was to look at all the homes, then go back to our motel room and make a decision, the rationale being that our reserve would give us a stronger negotiating position, since the realtor represents the seller.

After looking at four or five unsuitable locations (houses jammed next to each other—definitely not the feeling we were looking for), we drove down a secluded lane onto a peninsula with only two houses on that side of the lake. Dave got out of the car and started jumping up and down, yelling "This is it! This is it!" without even looking at the house. So much for subtlety.

Even though it is 400 feet of lakefront property, we paid less than half of what it would have cost in Texas and less than 10 percent of prices in Lake Tahoe. We were able to sell one of our cars, we had less need for a closet-full of stylish clothing, and we found pleasure in simple things that don't break a budget. The pace of life is more peaceful, the scenery more tranquil, and the potential for long-term friendships stronger than anywhere we have lived in the past. And the girls feel a sense of permanence, knowing where "home" is and probably will be for some time.

A HOME WITH A VIEW

We have been living in our secluded "state-park" setting for a year now. The wildlife have kept us entertained throughout the year. In the spring, Kathy often sits at our kitchen table looking lakeward from the window. In one swoop, her eyes might take in deer feeding in the early morning mist; Canadian geese swimming along with their three babies; a swallow feeding her newly hatched young; chipmunks and baby squirrels scurrying about; fish throwing themselves out of the water, forming a pattern of circular ripples on the lake; a wood duck with eight fuzzy offspring waddling behind; a beaver drawing a V-shaped design as he maneuvers through the water; mallards lazily exploring our peninsula; and a heron spearing a fish and flying off again. Out another window, we can see numerous turtles warming themselves on a fallen log next to the apple trees and grape vines. On some days we might even catch a glimpse of wild swans floating near our dock.

In addition to making the major move to a less-expensive location, we have been downscaling in other areas that will be covered in subsequent chapters. We are not saying that in order to downscale you have to make the same decisions we did. What we will offer is a blueprint you can use to help you begin where you are and perhaps to help you to determine what is right for your situation.

We are reaping the rewards of downscaling—a closer, happier family unit; a strengthened marriage; less stress; less overhead; a greater hope for the future; an opportunity to help others get out of the strangling rat-race existence; and a sense of security in finally being able to develop roots through community involvement and friendships. It is our desire that by using this book as a resource and encouragement, you too will be able to experience deeper relationships and more fulfillment in who you are and in the work you have chosen to do.

Castles
for Sale

PART 2

4

Urban Castles to Rural Cottages

Sitting in the mindless stop-and-go chain of honking horns, choking on poisonous exhaust fumes, we gave thanks that we were aliens to the scene. Years earlier we had lived in the Los Angeles area for a short time. As you become desensitized to and numbed by traffic aggravation, you learn to take it in stride, and we were no exception. Now, after living without this major time-waster and nerve specialty, and then being jolted into the system once again, we appreciated the full impact of the meaning of rush-hour traffic.

If traffic of that sort is your daily fare, perhaps you identify with these feelings: "Maybe it will happen while you're lounging on the beach. Or drinking in the night air and the stars on the porch of a mountain cabin. Or visiting friends in a town where ten minutes is considered a long commute and the kids bike-pool themselves to baseball practice."[1] "It" is a touch of wistful longing for simpler times and more meaningful friendships. "It" is a yearning for an escape from modern pressures brought on by pockets of overpopulation. "It" is the courage to make hard choices for the good of your family.

LOOKING HARD AT URBAN LIFE

All of us have a natural desire for inner satisfaction. We long for our lives to have a deeper level of meaning. At one time this yearning took many of us to the cities—the hub of corporate America

—looking for fulfillment to the exclusion of relationships, service, or worship. Now we are reconsidering, rethinking, and reevaluating.

David Meer, a senior vice president at Daniel Yankelovich Group, Inc., a market research firm, reports that "the search for community, safety, and meaning will preoccupy boomers in the 1990's."[2] That search for community is leading to a developing awareness of less urban lifestyles. Borne out of desperation or dissatisfaction, a new openness to country life has developed among many Americans.

This reevaluation is not necessarily a complete rejection of the cities, but it is an openness to change in the way things have been done. "Most of us have no interest in forsaking everything we have worked for to live out a romantic ideal in the woods. What we do long for is a middle ground: a place where the modern conveniences and intellectual and professional challenges of big-city life do not take us over but merely give our lives depth; where the cost of living does not force us to give up our own happiness to meet a monthly mortgage payment; and where success has a more personal meaning than continually moving ahead in a job."[3]

Cities do have advantages. Most Americans would give higher ratings to cities in the following areas: "Better public transportation, arts and cultural activities, better public schools, better police protection, entertainment, and better health care services. Sometimes what constitutes a 'better' service or amenity is largely subjective."[4] Those living in large cities are thought to have more daily tensions and pressure, yet they are also considered to be more accepting of the opinions of others.[5]

Yet with all the amenities cities have to offer, as the century progresses the negatives are outweighing the positives.

The anxious mood intensifies in the largest cities. Desperation escalates when people feel as though they are prisoners of their circumstances. Charles Kuralt noted on ABC's "World News Tonight" (July 10, 1992) that "Sixty percent of those polled in New York City would move if they could. . . . Fifty percent said the quality of life was 'hellish.'"

Those who can are getting out—out of a system where personal worth is dependent upon outward adornment and the facade of wealth; out of a climate of greed, fear, distrust, worry, hostility, and hate; out of exposure to harmful environments, both emotional and

physical. Amy Saltzman writes in her timely book, *Downshifting,* "What . . . mass movements to the country . . . tell us . . . is that people are searching, no matter how awkwardly, for options beyond cookie-cutter urban professionalism. An underlying theme seems to fuel most urban escapees: it is a belief that the high prices, honking horns and impatient tenor of urban and suburban life have pushed them further and further away from the sense of neighborhood and community found in small-town America."[6]

THE LONG COMMUTE

Every day, over 90 million solitary commuters are on America's highways and another 10 million carpool with others.[7] "Traffic congestion has increased in metropolitan areas nationwide, and commuters, families, and organizations are absorbing the associated hidden costs."

The writer of a *Wall Street Journal* profile of a town in California observed that many residents spent a minimum of two hours one way commuting to jobs in Los Angeles, sometimes even three hours if "an accident ties up traffic on the Pomona Freeway. It is not unusual for a resident of Moreno Valley to commute 4 to 6 hours each weekday."[8] Steve Farrar, commenting on this report in his book *If I'm not Tarzan and My Wife Isn't Jane, What Are We Doing in the*

Jungle? puts those figures into perspective: "Think of it. That's one-sixth of your life, not working, but going to work. That's nuts! That's crazy! That's . . . that's . . . idiotic!"[9]

It *is* idiotic, and it is harmful to your health. Traffic congestion "operates as a behavioral constraint on movement and goal attainment, thus constituting an adversive, frustrating condition. Our research has found that high-impedance commuting has adverse effects on blood pressure, mood, frustration tolerance, illness occasions, work absences, job stability, and overall life satisfaction," says Raymond W. Novaco, in an article discussing the consequences of commuting.[10]

THE LIVABILITY FACTOR

Have we had enough yet? "The current reawakening of environmental concerns is drawing many out of metropolitan hibernation," say Marilyn and Tom Ross in *Country Bound*™. People "are tired of polluted air, tainted water, dangerous landfills, littered streets, and blaring ghetto blasters. They want natural, quietly unsullied surroundings—to walk a gentle path. To reach that goal many are heading for a rural setting."[11]

If that's not enough to consider relocating to a smaller area, consider this: "Urban life has a tendency to make kids conceited, self-centered, and exploitative. Many demand expensive techie toys, rebel against doing chores and being responsible, and insist on hanging out with friends who give their parents the creeps. Country kids have a different lifestyle. Rather than staring glued to the television, they're more likely to be outdoors doing something adventuresome."[12]

An increase in environmental-related illnesses, smog, toxic waste dumps, excessive crime, and escalating costs all add up to low marks for the quality of life. Results of a test from Pepperdine University called "Lifegain" suggest that country dwellers live longer than their counterparts in the city.[13]

William Seavey, in a press release issued by the Greener Pastures Institute, notes that "an increasing body of evidence" suggests "that there is an outside limit to how large cities can grow and still maintain their livability. Several experts and researchers say that communities with the most balanced quality of life in America today are mid-sized, 50,000 to 250,000 population. These cities are somewhat distant from other cities so as to have fewer what I call urban spillover problems like smog and freeway traffic."[14]

CALIFORNIA EXODUS

Nowhere are the detrimentals of urban living more noticeable than in California. At one time life in California epitomized "the good life," but now Californians are realizing that it may not be that good after all. Earthquakes, major fires, droughts, floods, drive-by shootings, toxic wastes, raw sewage, insects that destroy crops, gang violence, riots, government regulations, high taxes, influx of illegal immigrants, and possible loss of libraries and preventative health care have paved the way to an exodus eastward.[15] California has the third highest sales tax in the nation, 8.25 percent, and one of the highest per capita income taxes.[16] "If current trends continue, there will be only four taxpayers for every five recipients of state assistance by the year 2,000."[17] Businesses are leaving. "A survey by the California Business Roundtable showed that nearly a quarter of the companies in [California] plan to leave."[18]

Other states have noticed this trend and are courting California businesses to wed with their economies. The hope of additional revenue and employment offers economically strapped states the motivation to develop programs, offer tax breaks, and attractively present their states as a viable option for a business union with California's merchants and manufacturers.

Midsized towns are also trying to import workers from major cities. Sioux Falls, South Dakota, for example, with a population of just over 100,000, has an unemployment rate one-third the national average. They have so many jobs available that they advertise for workers in newspapers from depressed cities.[19]

Lack of confidence in urban life is evident in the private sector, too. Truck rentals for moving household goods are doing well in California as more and more residents are heading east.[20] People are leaving for reasons of lifestyle and finances. The average-priced home in California is $200,000.[21] Yet as Lani Luciano observes in *Money* magazine, whereas "the cost of living varies as much as 90% from the most expensive parts of the country (California and the Northeast) to the least expensive (Florida and Texas), salaries seldom vary by more than 25%. According to the Economic Research

Institute in Newport Beach, California, someone earning $48,000 a year in Los Angeles would typically take no more than a 13% pay cut by moving to Atlanta, yet his cost of living would drop by more than half."[22]

In the past, California's lure was its mild climate, propensity to the ocean, opportunity, growth, and beauty. With many of these features either destroyed or marred in recent years, California has lost some of its attraction. Indeed, for many who live there, the state's vices offset the benefits that originally enticed them to the place. Because of the earlier migration west, California now hosts seven of the ten most expensive areas of housing in the United States. Honolulu, New York, and Boston are the other three. (The least expensive areas in the country include Salt Lake City; Denver; Houston; Oklahoma City; Dallas-Ft. Worth; Kansas City, Missouri; Indianapolis; Milwaukee; Richmond, Virginia; and Atlanta.)[23]

DECIPHERING FACTUAL REALITIES

The 1992 total cost of goods and services for a family of four, including food-at-home, food-away-from-home, tobacco, alcohol, furnishings and household operations, clothing, domestic services, medical care, personal care, recreation, and sales tax, in the most expensive areas were Manhattan, $22,120; Honolulu, $20,068; Washington, D.C., $18,430.

The totals for the least expensive areas were San Antonio, Texas, $15,460; Billings, Montana, $15,476; and Escanaba, Michigan, $15,585.[24]

Other factors enter into the financial picture. Those areas with high real estate taxes include Battle Creek, Michigan; Racine, Wisconsin; and Syracuse, New York. The lowest tax areas are Monroe, Louisiana; Decatur, Alabama; and Honolulu, Hawaii. (Keep in mind that an equivalent home in Monroe, Louisiana, costing $106,000 would have a price tag of $465,400 in Honolulu. It is the percentage of the home market value that reflects the lower tax.)[25] The average cost of country living on an annual basis is $23,106 versus $28,584 in urban areas.[26]

Then there are environmental concerns and crime. The three cities in America with the cleanest, driest air are Sedona, Arizona; Boulder City, Nevada; and Greeley, Colorado. The healthiest states, according to the Northwest National Life Insurance Company, are predominantly rural: Utah, North Dakota, Idaho, Vermont, Nebraska, Colorado, Wyoming, and Montana.[27]

The five safest areas, according to the Department of Justice, are Grand Forks and Bismarck, North Dakota; Eau Claire, Wisconsin; Parkersburg-Marietta, West Virginia; and Saint Cloud, Minnesota. The highest crime areas are New York City; Miami-Hialeah; Los Angeles-Long Beach, California; Jacksonville, Florida; and Flint, Michigan.[28]

It is interesting to note the difference in costs from 1991 to 1992 in the median price of a home in various cites across the United States. Those figures indicate a trend in the health of local economies. Cities that have experienced positive growth include Cedar Rapids, Iowa (+16.8 percent); Richland-Kennewick, Washington (+16.1 percent); and Saginaw, Michigan (+15.8 percent). On the other hand, Philadelphia (-8.9 percent); Miami (-6.6 percent); and New Haven, Connecticut (-6.2 percent) have experienced negative growth. For the country as a whole the average price of a home increased 1.6 percent to $103,500.[29]

JANE'S STORY

Jane grew up in Buffalo and graduated from college when she was twenty. She disliked the weather in the northeast and headed for the sun, first living in Mexico City, then New Orleans, and finally San Diego. By this time she was married, and concern for their children caused Jane and her husband, Chuck, to contemplate their situation. They were adverse to raising their two daughters, ages six and eight, in an environment of fast lane, hectic living; long commutes; expensive housing and subsequent maintenance; day-care centers; car expenses and more maintenance.

The seeds of change were planted when they returned to Buffalo in May of 1990 for a high school reunion. Up to this point, Jane and Chuck had never thought about Small Town, U.S.A. They had taken for granted that they needed to live in at least a large town, but not necessarily a huge town, because of their jobs.

Then, after exploratory trips to New York, in July of that year Jane quit her job in California without another on the horizon. She traveled to New York and stayed with a friend while going through the process of buying a house in a town of about fifteen thousand in the state's picturesque Finger Lakes region.

Chuck accepted a position in New York state as a computer programmer at two-thirds of the salary he earned in San Diego. While finishing out his thirty day's notice period at work, he was able to be on-site throughout the process of disposing of their two houses in Southern California.

It took Jane almost five months to land a suitable position, but she is now a contract technical writer. Originally, the company wanted her to be an employee, but she convinced them to permit her to work from home. Although she pays additional taxes and has no benefits (she is covered under Chuck's insurance), she has freedom not available in the corporate structure. And she hopes to make $50,000 this year. With Chuck's $60,000 annual salary, their actual earnings will be $5,000 a year more than they were in San Diego. But the biggest financial advantage is the 40 percent reduction in their living expenses.

It has now been two years since Chuck and Jane made "The Big Move." In their words, they "absolutely love it!" They confess it is hard to find any drawbacks, except maybe the long drive to get some good Mexican food. Jane also misses dressing up for Christmas parties. And although they enjoy the seasons, the winter weather is dreary compared to the sun in San Diego. But Jane is quick to add that the quality of life is the best they have ever enjoyed. The benefits of raising their children in a value-oriented climate far exceed the loss of additional days in the sun. The people in their small town are helpful and friendly, and there are great schools for kids. They have more time together to maintain and enjoy family closeness. Their overriding sentiment is that they wish they had made the move a long time ago.[30]

NOTES

1. Janet Bodnar and Kevin McManus, "Kissing the Big City Good-bye," *Changing Times,* August 1990, 27.

2. Quoted in Marilyn Ross and Tom Ross, *Country Bound!™ Trade Your Business Suit Blues for Blue Jean Dreams™* (Buena Vista, Colo.: Communication Creativity, 1992), 15. All quotes from this work are used by permission.

3. Amy Saltzman, *Downshifting: Reinventing Success on a Slower Track* (New York: HarperCollins, 1991), 176.

4. The Roper Organization, Inc., *Public Attitudes Toward Rural America And Rural Electric Cooperatives* (June 1992), 38.

5. Ibid, 40.

6. Amy Saltzman, *Downshifting: Reinventing Success on a Slower Track* (New York: HarperCollins, 1991), 174.

7. Dwight Hooten, *Have a Good Day* 25, no. 6 (Ocober 1992), 3.

8. "What's News," *Wall Street Journal,* 25 October 1990, 1.

9. Steve Farrar, *If I'm not Tarzan and My Wife Isn't Jane, What Are We Doing in the Jungle?* (Portland, Oreg.: Multnomah, 1991), 24–25.

10. Raymond W. Novaco, "Home Environmental Consequences of Commute Travel Impedance," *American Journal of Community Psychology* 19, no. 6 (1991), 881–82.

11. Ross and Ross, 17

12. Ross and Ross, 27

13. William Seavey, "Bits and Pieces," *Greener Pastures Gazette* 5, no. 2 (Spring 1992), 5.

14. William Seavey, Greener Pastures Institute press release, 1 November 1992, 2.

15. Richard Price and Maria Goodavage, "Golden State Loses Some Luster," *USA Today,* 10 July 1992, 4A.

16. Rowland Evans and Robert Novak, "California: Paradise Lost?" *Reader's Digest,* April 1992, 56.

17. Ibid., 58.

18. Ibid., 55.

19. Patricia Edmonds, "Economic Extremes: Forward vs. Poorward," *USA Today,* 17 February 1992, 4A.

20. "Investment Update/California Crisis," *Kiplinger's Personal Finance Magazine,* November 1992, 26.

21. Evans and Novak, 55.

22. Lani Luciano, "How to Cut Your Expenses 20% (and Live Better Too)," *Money,* December 1991, 73.

23. Bill Montague, "Realty Gridlock Slow to Break," *USA Today,* 31 January 1992, 4B.

24. Runzheimer International [Rochester, Wis.], *Consumer's Digest,* September 1992, 12.

25. Ibid., 8.

26. William Seavey, "Costs of Country Living," *Greener Pastures Gazette* 4, no. 4 (Fall 1991), 3. The reference in Seavey's article is to a study reported in *American Demographics* magazine.

27. Ross and Ross, 18.

28. Ibid., 17.

29. National Association of Realtors, "Median Home Prices Across the US," *USA Today,* 16 November 1992, 4B.

30. Taken from a telephone interview. Used by permission.

5

Moving to "Mayberry, U.S.A."

om, my rabbit is missing!" Kimberly yelled in the door shortly after going outside to feed her pet. All three girls had rab-
bits they had showed at the Alaska State Fair for 4-H. They
had even won ribbons. All three had grown emotionally attached to their pets. Now Kimberly was frantically trying to find
hers in the dense growth that surrounded our home in a somewhat
secluded area with a panoramic view.

Running out with her slippers still on, Kathy joined in the
search. Across the road she thought she caught a glimpse of something moving in the woods. Making a dash for the bushes, she spied
a mousy brown rabbit that looked like Kimberly's. With the rabbit
about ten feet away, Kathy began the chase. Around trees and
bushes, over logs and under limbs, finally Kathy was gaining. Only a
few more feet and she would have him. As she lunged forward,
about to close both hands around the furry body, Kimberly yelled
from our yard, "Mom, never mind! The rabbit's still in the cage!"
Kathy quickly jerked her hands back, only inches away from snag-
ging a wild rabbit. It seems that Kimberly's rabbit had been huddled
all along in a dark corner of its large cage. Kimberly had simply pan-
icked when her pet failed to greet her in its usual manner.

Many of us give chase to ambition, power, wealth, or prestige.
And just as we are about to grasp it (or for that matter, even after
we have it in hand), we find it's a "wild rabbit" and the more important one is safe at home after all.

Are you caught up in a wild rabbit chase while ignoring your family at home? Perhaps you feel trapped in a dead-end street, constrained by your environment, choked by your commitments, and chained by deteriorating relationships. Not that you need a change *from* your relationships, but rather a change *toward* them. By alleviating unnecessary stressors that go hand-in-hand with city living and working, you could free yourself to more fully enjoy those same relationships.

Perhaps you've come to the conclusion that a change is necessary—a change that will help you to put your family back into its proper place in your life. You may even have decided to move to a smaller community. If so, as we have already seen, you are one of a growing number who are exchanging "only existing" in the fast-lane for "really living" in the slower lane. If not, you may be wondering, *What is the attraction of small towns, and why should I consider this alternative?*

The exodus to small towns is in contrast to the pattern of emigration from rural to urban areas that began in the 1820s and continued through the 1960s and 1970s, usually the result of people pursuing higher salaries. In recent decades 3 million more Americans moved to the country than to metro areas. For those who moved long distances, there was a decrease of from 70 to 50 percent in the number of people who were packing their bags in search of higher pay.[1]

More and more Americans are refocusing their energies—away from financial rewards and closer to emotional ones; away from being controlled by advertisers' messages and closer to listening to their families; away from personal selfishness and closer to concern for others.

The Roper Organization says of this migration: "Widespread pessimism about the future of the nation, and to a lesser extent, of their community, may be causing the public to lower its personal expectation about attaining financial success. More important than rising from rags to riches, majorities simply say freedom to live life as they choose and to have enough money to enjoy their leisure are essential."[2]

THE ESCAPE

Whereas once we could have counted on a country that followed the values of our founding fathers, now we have to be wary of legislation that destroys those same values. Whereas once our country upheld a spirit of community, now we live in a country that often embraces discord and disunity. (Even though those who embrace discord are a minority, that minority creates the illusion of being a majority.) Whereas once economic growth could see no limit, now we are faced with the stark reality: there is indeed a limit.

More than three-fourths of the American public say our country is headed in the wrong direction. This reflects the most discouraging national mood in twenty years.[3] "Not only does the public see the American Dream fading, but most Americans also feel this country is starting to lose its 'traditional values.'"[4]

The undercurrent of desire to escape large populated areas in favor of settings that offer more tranquillity may be an effort to recapture some of what we have lost. Some studies have shown that as many as 40 percent of those living in big cities actually would prefer to live in a smaller community.[5] "Other popular choices are a medium size city (21%) or a suburban area (also 21%), and 16% would like to live in a small city."[6]

Most are seeking the collective advantages of rural living. Those advantages are most likely found in unique subdivisions near large cities, in small communities far from the hustle and bustle of urban areas, or on sprawling lands just outside a midsized city. "Only a fraction of the population (13%) technically resides in population areas that most would consider rural (country areas of 35,000 or less). However, 33% claim to currently live in a rural locale, including a fraction of residents of major metropolitan areas and other non-rural locations. The designation of 'rural' for some Americans seems to be subjective—an indication, perhaps, of remoteness from neighbors or conveniences or maybe a peaceful, non-urban setting."[7]

MAYBERRY'S ATTRACTION

One friend who made the move from a city to a small town wrote,

Small towns have a strong sense of community, perhaps as a result of stable family roots—there is not as much uprooting as in urban areas. People pull together. There is drift away from the "yuppie mentality." After moving, I felt more freedom from the pressure to be "on top of it" socially, materially, etc. We have found small-town living is slower paced for a better family life. Events and places are simply geographically closer and it seems to make a difference. In a small community one is forced to handle problems more concretely. It seems as if when living in a highly populated city, it is easier to hide or escape from problems. For instance in a city, if I have a church problem, I simply go to another church. In a small town one doesn't have that option! If there are business problems, one must handle them promptly because of high visibility.

Small towns offer a sense of organization and manageability that translates into more personal control. Responsibility and accountability build character and a richer life. The educational systems, by virtue of their size and limited exposure to modern vices, can devote more time to teaching than to combatting negative cultural distractions.

The Roper Organization observes: "No other Americans are as satisfied and as enthusiastic about their communities as are rural Americans; the grass is not greener on the other side of the fence. Rural Americans appear to be truly proud of their communities and satisfied with their lifestyle; they are the only Americans who would choose overwhelmingly to stay put even if they had the chance to move to another location."[8]

Small-town people as a whole are often friendlier, hold on to traditional values, and lead less stress-filled lives, appreciating nature and simpler ways. Even if they don't recognize you in a store, they still trust you with an out-of-town check. When we were new to the area where we now live, Dave needed to rent a trailer for a day. On the basis of a gentleman's agreement, he took the trailer home. There was no contract and the owner didn't know Dave. A suspicious mentality is absent from most small towns, and living in fear is a foreign emotion for the average person. People are kinder and more helpful. Kathy locked her keys in our van recently. Fifteen minutes later, through the help of several townspeople, she was on her way.

Marilyn and Tom Ross observe in *Country Bound*™ that "qualities once taken for granted—trust and honesty, regional and ethnic heritage, clean air and friendly neighbors—are special treasures. As the news highlights the emerging global economy, many of us simply hunger for a supportive local network. We need to feel connected. . . . Along with quietude comes a simpler lifestyle. Wearing apparel is more functional, less glitzy. Escargot and oysters on the half shell give way to meat loaf and mashed potatoes. Pickup trucks outnumber snazzy sports cars. Entertainment centers around people rather than places. Religious ties are stronger and the church often plays a social as well as spiritual role. Parades, band concerts, and school events replace ballet, opera, and gallery openings."[9] For those who do want more elite cultural outlets from time to time, most rural areas are located less than a two-hour drive from a larger city.

OTHER ADVANTAGES

Although character qualities are valued in rural residents, more than 70 percent of all Americans polled named these advantages as well: "The cost of living, personal values, traffic conditions, freedom from pollution, community spirit, and a better overall quality of life."[10]

Stated in another way, a majority of rural Americans rate their communities good to excellent on fifteen out of eighteen elements of community life: Personal values (86%), community or civic spirit (85%), overall quality of life (81%), traffic conditions (81%), friendliness of people (75%), condition of streets and roads (69%), freedom from pollution (65%), cost of living (62%), recreational facilities (62%), available health care services (61%), police protection (60%), privacy (60%), job opportunities (57%), availability of entertainment (52%), and a place to raise children (51%). A near majority (49%) say their public schools rate good to excellent."[11]

RURALITE DEFINED

There are other differences between country folk and city folk. According to two surveys taken by the Roper Organization, 50 percent of those living in rural areas hold to religious beliefs whereas only 13 percent of those living in urban areas do. Fifty-eight percent of ruralites versus 5 percent of urbanites have a commitment to the community. Sixty-nine percent of people from rural areas compared to 4 percent of urban dwellers consider family to be very important. "Rural Americans are also perceived to be healthier, more honest, and more capable of enjoying life. . . . 35% of Americans say they would like to be living in rural areas in 10 years."[12]

Just who is this breed of rural American? The profile of an average rural American would be a conservative, registered voter with a lower than average income (a yearly average of $25,200 compared with $31,200 for the nation as a whole) and is likely to be what the Roper Organization calls an "Influential American." "Influential Americans are those citizens who are more inclined to action and involvement. They do something about the issues that concern them as both consumers and as citizens."[13] Forty-eight percent of rural Americans live in the south, whereas 34 percent claim the Midwest as their home.[14]

People may go about their quest for their "dream town" in different ways. *USA Today* ran a letter from a reader in San Diego (February 21, 1992) who expressed a desire for a town where people cared about each other and the locale was picturesque, where there was a low crime rate, and that had a local park where summer concerts could be heard. The letter-writer urged other readers to let him know if such a town existed. A few days later some of the responses were printed. Readers boasted of caring, friendly towns in several different states. There are similar towns all across the country, away from the hassles of big cities where 17 percent of America's land area contains 83 percent of her population.[15]

William L. Seavey notes in *Greener Pastures Gazette* that "James Rouse, a noted urban planner, contends that large cities are so huge they prevent people from feeling in control of their lives. 'I believe this out-of-scaleness promotes loneliness, irresponsibility, and superficial values. People grow best in small communities where the institutions, which are dominant forces in their lives, are within the scale of their comprehension and within reach of their sense of responsibility and capacity to manage.'"[16]

GETTING TO MAYBERRY

Suppose you want to make the transition from urban to country living but would like to look at resources that would make the journey easier. Are such resources available? There are indeed.

An excellent resource for anyone seriously considering relocating is a book written by Marilyn and Tom Ross, *Country Bound!™ Trade Your Business Suit Blues for Blue Jean Dreams™*.

> [*Country Bound!™*] shows disgruntled urbanites how to effectively escape the big city rat race, create a successful business in the boonies, and experience an enhanced quality of life.
>
> A business book as well as a lifestyle guide, it details how to earn a good living in Small Town America. Readers discover ways to turn avocational pastimes into regular paychecks—telecommute to their existing jobs—set up an "information age" home-based business—buy an existing rural enterprise—create their dream job in the country. Dozens of maps, tables, quizzes, and checklists make relocating easy and fun.[17]

Relocating is never easy (remember our forty-five moves?), but this volume will certainly make it easier for you. The 433-page trade paperback is $19.95, plus $3.00 shipping. It can be ordered directly from Communication Creativity, Box 1500DS, Buena Vista, CO 81211; (800) 331-8355.

Who might be interested in *Country Bound!™*? Disenchanted baby boomers, men going through male menopause, owners of home-based businesses, telecommuters, retirees, parents wanting a safe environment for their children, and those considering purchasing a vacation home.[18]

Another resource that helps urban Americans relocate to smaller cities and towns in rural and recreational areas is a newsletter called *Greener Pastures Gazette,* published by the Greener Pastures Institute. The *Gazette* encourages "living that is simpler and more self-reliant with small town values and lifestyles" and is available by writing to the *Gazette* at P.O. Box 1122, Sierra Madre, CA 91025; (818) 355-1670 or (800) 688-9017. Former clients of Greener Pastures Institute who have made successful moves are part of a growing informal "hinterland host" network that advises (and sometimes lodges) prospective movers on issues relating to the host's community. One book we read about in the *Greener Pastures Gazette* is *How to Buy Land Cheap* by Edward Preston. It covers buying tax sale property from county, state, and federal agencies. Greener Pastures Institute reports that one woman purchased a two-story home in good condition in North Dakota for $500 using the information from this book.

"More than 20 percent of Americans relocate every year," says Cheri Fuller in "On the Move," an article in *Moody* magazine.[19] If you move, will it lead to a happier life or just another rung? Will it create closer family relationships or tear them down? Will the move be conducive to instilling and maintaining strong personal and family values, or will it place you and your children in compromising positions?

If a move is on the horizon for you, keep this buying and selling tip in mind: Only desperate sellers put their house on the market between Thanksgiving and Christmas. Although there are fewer houses to choose from if you are a buyer, you may be able to save thousands of dollars if you purchase a home during this season. On the other hand, be careful of creating a situation where you have to list your house during that same period. It is typical for housing prices to peak in August, bottom out in October and rise again in January.[20]

The newsletter *Caretaker Gazette,* Box 342, Carpentersville, IL 60110, could line you up with short-term caretaking or house-sitting positions from cabins to farming ventures. In this way you could check out an area before making a major commitment to move.[21]

Leisure Living, Box 890, Springfield, MO 65801; (800) 755-6555, will link you with videos on various communities. Also, check with the local Chamber of Commerce for brochures and videos of areas in which you are interested.

The Rural Property Bulletin, The National Marketplace for Rural Property, P.O. Box 4331, Prescott, AZ 86302, provides twenty-four pages of property or businesses in rural areas, most being for sale by owner.

For one family, getting away from the Houston megalopolis meant they could pursue a simpler, less expensive lifestyle. In exchange for their life in Houston they now own a three-bedroom ranch on five acres next to the Gradalupe River near Kerrville, Texas, a town with a population of twenty thousand. The family goes fishing, canoeing, and rafting together. And the schools are "conservative and safe, with small classes and teachers who have received national recognition."[22]

Right Choice® is a private research firm that "computes after tax cash flow of a move or job change for the first year. . . . The analysis is based upon numerous cost of living and tax variables from all geographical areas throughout the country." If you need help in determining the financial advisability of a move, perhaps the $190 fee the firm charges could save you money in the long run. What seems to be a good offer, may in fact be less than you are making now if you take geographical costs into consideration; 2 Long Avenue, Derry, New Hampshire 23038; (800) 872-2294.[23]

In your search, schools are likely to be a major concern. "Areas with a low cost of living don't necessarily have poor-quality schools. In San Antonio, for example, the cost of living is just 90% of the national average. But San Antonio's Alamo Heights Independent School District is ranked in the 97th percentile for quality among all districts in the nation. Alamo Heights parents get the best of both worlds—good schools and low living costs. . . . Other areas that combine high-quality school districts with low costs of living include Casper, Wyoming; Longview, Texas; Springfield, Missouri; Boise, Idaho; Sioux Falls, South Dakota; South Bend, Indiana; and Huntsville, Alabama."[24]

You may be considering relocating, whether it be across the country or across the county. How do you determine the feasibility of a school, either public or private? Which of the 598 public school systems in a sixty-mile radius of Trenton, New Jersey, would you be most pleased with? Which school most closely aligns itself to philosophies you consider important? If you have a child with special needs (disabled, gifted, or promising athletic ability), how do you go about finding schools that are the most compatible for that child?

SchoolMatch® has information on almost sixteen thousand public school systems and eight thousand private schools. The private schools may be in the United States or overseas. *SchoolMatch®* is a search firm that links you with schools according to your preferences of class/teacher ratios, accreditation (nationally, only one-fifth of all public schools are accredited), tuition, scholarships, competition, and curriculum. For $97.50 the organization will provide you with the top fifteen schools and communities that most closely fit your preferences, with a scale showing how each school matches your expectations and/or needs; 5027 Pine Creek Drive, Blendonview Office Park, Westerville, OH 43081; (800) 992-5323.[25]

There seems to be a wealth of magazines springing up that cater to those who want to lead a simpler life, are looking for meaning and a sense of specialness about living, or who have tried "the good life" and found it lacking, disappointing, and at times even destructive. From the way advertisers slant their ads to the selection of stories the media chooses to cover, the trend back to the country is gaining momentum. And as more and more Americans realize there is a viable alternative to urban life, our nation is finally beginning the slow, arduous ascent to developing closer family ties and more satisfying relationships.

Ask yourself what you really want and how much less are you willing to settle for in competing and conflicting areas in order to achieve a simpler, more fulfilling life. Perhaps the first step for you is to consider your options in one area of the country, determine the radius from a large city hub that you would be comfortable with, and begin your search within that boundary. Moving to a less-populated area does not mean giving up your career completely. Maybe it only means pursuing a less intense career path so that you can more enjoy your work and your family.

All of life involves choices and trade-offs. We forego a new car this year to help with a son's college tuition. We nix the movie tonight in favor of visiting friends. We turn down that promotion because it would mean more time away from home. We give up a quiet evening to watch a daughter cheer at a basketball game. If we look at our decisions as choices rather than forced compliance, our attitude changes and frees us from resentment. However, if we dwell on the downside of a situation, anger and bitterness can easily take over. There is always a worse scenario than the one we are presently in. Appreciate the positives while changing what you can about the negatives. More than likely we are where we are because of choices we have made. And it will be by choice that we either change our outlook or the situation itself. But for you, the beginning of a better future may lie in making the move to "Mayberry, U.S.A."

NOTES

1. William L. Seavey, "Back to the Land in the Nineties," *New Realities* (March/April 1991), 36.

2. The Roper Organization, Inc., *Public Attitudes Toward Rural America and Rural Electric Cooperatives* (June 1992), 5. A study conducted for National Rural Electric Cooperative Association. Quotes are used by permission.

3. Ibid., 7.

4. Ibid., 11.

5. William L. Seavey, "City Dwellers Want to Move," *Greener Pastures Gazette* 4, no. 4 (Fall 1991), 1. (Referring to a study in *Demography Magazine,* November 1990.)

6. Roper, 34.

7. Ibid., 32.

8. Roper, 81.

9. Marilyn Ross and Tom Ross, *Country Bound!*™ *Trade Your Business Suit Blues for Blue Jean Dreams* (Buena Vista, Colo.: Communication Creativity, 1992), 15, 18. All quotes from this work are used by permission. To order the 433-page trade paperback send $19.95 plus $3.00 shipping to: Communication Creativity, Box 1500DS, Buena Vista, CO 81211; (800) 331-8355.

10. Roper, vi.

11. Ibid., viii.

12. Michelle Seebach, "Small Towns Have a Rosy Image," *American Demographics* 14, no. 10 (October 1992), 19.

13. Roper, 79.

14. Ibid., 80.

15. William L. Seavey, "You Can't Eat Scenery: Making a Living in the Countryside" *Greener Pastures Gazette*, Special Report (October 1991), 1.

16. William Seavey, "Quote of the Issue," *Greener Pastures Gazette* 5, no. 1 (Winter 1992), 3.

17. Hugh Goding, "Millions Prepare to Participate in Silent Revolution," news release. Golding can be reached at (719) 395-2459.

18. Ross and Ross, 4–5.

19. Cheri Fuller, "On the Move," *Moody*, September 1991, 30.

20. Lani Luciano, "How to Cut Your Expenses 20% (and Live Better Too)," *Money,* December 1991, 81–82.

21. Ross and Ross, 105.

22. Janet Bodnar and Kevin McManus, "Kissing the Big City Good-bye," *Changing Times,* August 1990, 31.

23. *Right Choice*®. Brochure, 1.

24. Nancy Ten Kate, "Good Schools and Low Living Costs," *American Demographics* 14, no. 3 (March 1992); reprinted by SchoolMatch.

25. SchoolMatch promotional material.

6

Crosstown Transplants

It was the American Dream. For Robert and Cindy, the long months of planning, overseeing, and waiting had now come to an end. Daily they trekked to their secluded lot to observe the progress of the builders. Each time another phase of the project was completed, they imagined anew how wonderful it would be to actually live in their dream home.

Finally, they moved from their small rental into their very own 2,500 square foot, cedar-sided home. They would both have to work long hours to be able to make the payments, but they had arrived. Their home boasted affluence inside and out. The landscaping was tailored to present just the right image. Inside, all of the latest appliances graced the kitchen and laundry areas. Fashionable wallpaper throughout highlighted the expensive molding and cabinets. The plush carpeting, real marble floors, spa, and two atriums added considerably to the builder's package, but they thought it would be worth it when their friends and families expressed their admiration.

During those first few months of excitement, using their many credit cards, Robert and Cindy bought new furnishings that created a home fit for high-gloss magazines. They also took out a hefty loan to buy an existing retail business—fulfilling yet another of their dreams. And the year before Cindy had bought a new car. She was the first in their circle of friends to have talking reminders to turn off the lights or take the keys out of the ignition.

Life for Robert and Cindy was the envy of many a couple. The only trouble was that this couple didn't count on the downside of the boom or bust economy of Alaska. As a result, their business didn't do as well as projected. And the collective credit card interest was increasing at a faster rate than their income could meet.

It had seemed so easy to acquire the new car, house, and furnishings. The salespeople were all congenial and had treated Robert and Cindy with respect, as if they were "somebody important." Because they had had a good credit record in the past, they were deemed a "good credit risk" in the present. Robert and Cindy had a twinge of discomfort from time to time in their spiral of acquisitions, but they salved their consciences by reaffirming their business income projections to each other. Also, Cindy was up for a promotion so they counted her expected hefty raise in their income reviews. But when Cindy was denied a raise in the midst of corporate downsizing, a sense of foreboding came over them.

To complicate their situation, since they were so tight on funds every month, they never got around to paying their estimated self-employment taxes. They figured they could catch up the next quarter. Besides, how would the government really know what they had made anyway?

Eventually things caught up with them. Not only did Cindy and Robert have to call a halt to impulse and extravagant buying, but they got further and further behind on monthly utilities, credit card payments, medical and car insurance, and miscellaneous bills that taunted them from the desk drawer. Each month it became a juggling act of which bill and what portion to pay.

Finally, the collection agencies started calling. They showed no mercy in their language and threats. So maybe it was good when the telephone company disconnected the phone.

Robert and Cindy didn't even bother to open the certified letters anymore. Their arguments about finances increased to the point where their debt was consuming them emotionally. Instead of working together to find a solution, they abused each other verbally.

From this point, it wasn't too long before the Internal Revenue Service caught up with them. Now the couple had to worry about back taxes, penalties, and interest. In the end, Robert and Cindy's dream evaporated: the business, their home, car, furnishings, and self-respect. Had their situation been handled differently at any number of points along the way, they could have avoided personal and financial devastation.

Even after having gone so far as to have the house built and then to move in, they still might have been able to reverse their downward slide. If they had put their dream home up for sale and moved to a more conservative neighborhood, they might have been able to salvage some of their dream in maintaining their newly acquired business. Even if they had to take a loss to get out of the steep house payments, in the end they might still have had something.

TRANSPLANTING

Moving to another area of town can reduce the cost of monthly house payments considerably. It used to be that Americans traded up as their equity in their homes grew over the years. In the '80s, young couples thought they "deserved it all" shortly after the wedding ceremony. The '90s are ripe for returning to the ways of one or two generations past. When the expenses connected with a house take up 40 percent of a couple's take-home pay, they will face extreme pressure if one income is severed or reduced.

It may be impractical for some people to move to another part of the country to take advantage of a lower cost of living. Family ties, secure employment, schooling, or friends may sway the decision to remain where they are despite the negatives of pollution, crime, high costs, and high population. But drastic changes may still be in order. Those changes may include selling their home in an affluent neighborhood and being content to relocate to a lower cost one.

Let's say that Robert and Cindy had decided to be content with less. If they had been able to sell their house in the fancy subdivision for what they paid for it, they would at least have come out even. But the greatest advantage would have come when they wrote the check each month for a 1,200 square-foot house. Instead of the $1,500 a month payment on a new house they would now have to pay only $650 a month on a fixer-upper. Their utilities would also have decreased proportionally.

While Cindy was still working, they could have applied the difference in house payments toward making credit card payments, paying their taxes, and catching up on other bills. Furthermore, they would not have needed so much furniture. Some could be sold, even at a loss, to help reduce their debt ratio. And if they had been serious

about getting out of their financial mess, Cindy could have sold her newer car and settled for an older one. (If you think this is drastic, remember that in the end they lost it all anyway!)

UNDERSTANDING THE NUMBERS

Dave sat down with a loan officer recently to work through a hypothetical scenario of an average cross-town transplant. Realtors fees, the deed, title work, and taxes to date constitute 8 to 10 percent of the selling cost for an existing home. For example, say you purchased a median house ten years ago for $100,000 that is now valued at $125,000 with $80,000 remaining on the mortgage. That means with selling expenses averaging $12,500, and with paying off the existing mortgage, you would have a balance of $32,500 in equity. Payments based on an average of 10.5 percent on the $100,000 home would be $915 a month for principle and interest.

But if you bought a home for $70,000, out of the $32,500 equity you could use $8,000 to pay off your consumer debt and $1,500 to cover closing costs. That would leave you with $23,000 to use as a down payment. Your mortgage balance would then be $47,000. At 9 percent (reflecting lower interest rates of current months) a thirty-year loan would be $378 a month for principle and interest.

There's more. After paying for ten years on your first mortgage, you now have ten fewer earning years than before. In that case, you might be wise to take out a twenty-year mortgage rather than a thirty-year one. The monthly payments would be $422, leaving an excess of over $500 a month difference between the mortgage payment on the two homes. (Subsequent taxes would also be lower, adding to the savings.)[1]

One reason financial planners suggest using part of one's equity to pay off consumer debt in situations like the one outlined above is the exorbitant interest rates often charged on credit cards, car loans, department store cards, and loans on anything from furniture and appliances to electronic equipment and computers. In 1991, the consumer debt (specifically credit cards and auto loans) was $727.2 billion. In June of 1992, that debt had decreased to $719.6 billion, according to the Federal Reserve. Consumers are getting smart. They realize that with an average of $14,500 debt (excluding mortgage), the best return for their money is not to put it in any kind of investment, but to pay off their debt. Here's why: The average credit card interest is 17 percent. In order to earn as much on your money as you would if you paid off your debt, you would need to get a return of 25.9 percent from your investment if you are in the 31 percent tax bracket. That figure decreases to 21.1 percent if you are in the 15 percent tax bracket. You would be hard pressed to find an investment that yields that kind of return in today's financial climate, where money market accounts are earning 2.5 to 3.5 percent.[2]

ALTERNATIVES

Usually, even decreasing the size of your house by one bedroom can make a significant difference in your monthly payment. Perhaps selling your four-bedroom house and purchasing a three-bedroom home with an attached garage could give you the space you need at a lower mortgage. Later, when you are able, you could turn the garage into one or two bedrooms. Here, on the lake, for example, our 1000-square-foot home was adequate when only our high schooler lived with us. Last year, the other two girls moved back home while taking time off from college to pay for their tuition. We have a storage shed with a loft, affectionately known as "the barn," that Dave turned into a beautiful retreat for our oldest daughter. She has decorated it with flair and has a sense of being on her own, yet close to the family. Because she graduated at sixteen, attended college for a couple of years, and then worked as a live-in nanny for two more, it was important to her to renew family relationships, especially since Dave was gone much of her last year of high school.

Currently 54 percent of young adults ages eighteen to twenty-four live at home.[3] This seems to be a trend as a result of hard times. It is more difficult today for young adults to find employment adequate to enable them to be on their own financially. Sometimes economics are secondary to trying to capture some of the closeness society has stolen from this generation. With the abolition of much of the extended family and the sense of rootlessness pervasive in our culture, young adults may come to appreciate their immediate family on a different plane than when they were adolescents and teenagers.

Adult children are returning home more mature and independent, willing to contribute to the overall health and satisfaction of the family. Many have had a taste of being autonomous in our fast-paced culture and found it lacking in depth and meaning. In trying to sort out unanswered questions about their identity and sense of belonging, the purpose to and meaning of their lives, and the source of ultimate satisfaction and fulfillment, they are returning to their childhood island of comfort.

We as parents can have a healthy influence on our adult children during this period of searching. We can offer them unconditional love. We can be there to listen and guide, enabling them to find answers in an atmosphere of acceptance and warmth. The danger comes when our kids want to come back and just "veg" or escape responsibility for their lives. But even in this, wise parents can encourage maturity by setting up guidelines as a prerequisite of returning. Those guidelines might include finding a job and helping to contribute to family expenses. If employment in your area is weak or there are other extenuating circumstances, you might require them to get involved in some sort of volunteer service. They should also share home responsibilities, such as cooking and cleaning, in addition to doing their own laundry and rooms. This should not be a time of coming back home so Mom or Dad can pamper them. Rather, it should be a season of developing closer relationships that might not have been possible in the past—a second chance for the adult child (and his or her parents) to tie up loose ends before the child continues on with life through marriage or career or both.

Jeannette is very responsible, and we are thankful to be able to enjoy some belated happy times together with her that were not possible earlier because of Dave's career. Her sunny personality and numerous avenues of creativity make her a joy to be around. To some extent we feel we are enjoying the fruits of our labor over the years. (We hope we did some things right!)

Our middle daughter is busy planning her wedding. With only two bedrooms in the house, and with our business expanding, we needed both an extra bedroom and an office to get the desk, office supplies, and work area out of the living room. So Dave divided our two-car garage into a room for Kimberly and an office for us. In doing so, not only did we gain the necessary footage, but we added a good bit of equity to the house as well. If this home had had more square footage (finished) initially, our mortgage would have been more than we would have wanted to pay. And since we bought it more for the property than for the house, we knew we could remodel later.

In building the office we are participating in a wider trend. The demand for houses with an existing home office is increasing with each passing year. New dwellings are often designed with a home office as part of the master plan. Faith Popcorn, a well-known ana-lyzer of trends, predicts that home offices will be the "newest real estate development. As if in answer to that prediction, a recent *Denver Post* article quoted Andy Ades of Ades Design as saying, 'We're probably putting offices in more than half the homes we're building in the Evergreen (Colorado) area.'"[4] Channing Dawson, in an article in *The Practical Homeowner,* notes that because they must work "under two-earner time constraints and recessionally tight budgets, homeowners and their designers, architects, contractors and builders are coming up with smarter, more economical more ecologically viable . . . solutions."[5]

Perhaps some of your children are grown and you don't need as much space as in the past. By purchasing a smaller home, you could save thousands of dollars each year. Smaller houses lend them-selves to less yard work and cleaning, require fewer repairs, and afford less space in which to collect junk. There is a growing reper-toire of resources available that emphasize living more simply and less expensively. It is not chic anymore to try to "keep up with the Joneses," because the Joneses are deep in debt.

We are giving a six-week series on downscaling for a local church. After we had presented the benefits of moving across town, one couple shared their story. They now live in the inner city. In recent years an illness forced the wife to spend much time in a wheelchair. By selling their 1600-square-foot house and moving into a two-bedroom, 775-square-foot home, they have realized several advantages. First, from the equity built up in their other house and from the subsequent lower payments on the smaller home, they were able to pay off their current residence in three to four years.

Second, in a smaller home the wife can use a walker to get around instead of having to maneuver her wheelchair through the larger rooms. Third, they are closer to everything for convenience. Not only is it easier for to get to services and stores, but it is also more convenient for others to come and visit them—especially encouraging during down times of coping with a crippling illness.

"When we were younger we had to impress people. Now we just plan to live," the husband told us. "Being self-employed, I had no retirement. We are living comfortably and putting away for retirement at the same time." How many of us live where we do to make a good impression on others rather than to meet the needs of a family? How many of us would be willing to move across town to reduce the stress of providing for large house payments—taking us away from that house with no time to enjoy the family living there? How many of us are trading a building for the relationships that may be our only comfort in later years when our finances are depleted along with the physical strength to replenish them?

In *Living on Less and Liking It More,* Maxine Hancock observes: "Actually, our big ideas of housing reflect our growing accumulation of things far more than they show a real need of vast space for people. It is particularly ironic to consider that as houses get bigger, families get smaller."[6]

CHOICES AND CHANGES

Those who follow through and buy down to a smaller house will find that ensuing changes may take place. If they have school-age children who are not in a private school, their new school may be in a different district. Proximity to familiar shopping areas and immediate neighborhoods may change. The commute (hopefully) will be shorter and the taxes lower. If you choose a rural setting the drive may be longer, but it should be more serene. And you will realize another important consideration—the pressure resulting from hefty house payments will be reduced. In later chapters we will touch on how to better invest your potential excess of income than putting it into bricks and mortar.

In *If I'm Not Tarzan and My Wife Isn't Jane, What Are We Doing in the Jungle?* Steve Farrar describes an incident that reflects misplaced priorities. Following a speaking engagement, Steve spoke with a young mother who, in tears, told him how great a stress she was under. Putting her young son in day-care for ten to twelve hours a day while she worked full time was difficult for her, and she longed to be home with him. Later, Farrar says, the person taking him back to his hotel "stopped by a friend's home to drop off a package. We pulled up in front of a beautiful, brand-new house of at least 3,000 square feet. I found out later it had four bedrooms, a study, and three baths. Parked in the driveway was a new car in the $35,000–$40,000 range. As we drove into the driveway, you'll never guess who came walking out the front door. It was the young mother who just hours earlier had told me tearfully she would give anything to stay at home with her child. Here was a well-meaning and concerned Christian parent standing in front of a very large contradiction."[7]

SELLING YOUR HOME

A tip in getting ready to sell your home: people tend to pay more for a house that has the feeling of being well-kept. From manicured lawns and shrubs to working appliances, details can affect the outcome of the sale. Have a friend do an unbiased walk-through with you. Have them note those particulars that detract from the salability of your home. On the other hand, when buying a home, you will be able to save substantially on a house that needs lots of T.L.C. The cost of replacing or repairing is usually far less than the sum you would save as a result of some "sweat equity." New carpeting and fresh paint can do wonders for the home that carries a reduced price tag.

One doctor had come to a point in his life where he was consumed with bondage and boredom, time constraints and commitments. He even questioned the validity of his work actually making a difference. He was experiencing a crisis of meaning. His life with his family in a large home with a pool in an elite part of town had become too comfortable and selfish.

Then he responded to a challenge to give back to God a costly gift. For this doctor, the gift was the gift of being available. He and his wife sold their home and with the equity financed a trip to a medical center in Nairobi, Kenya. They were to spend a year filling in for a doctor on furlough. During the process of getting their family ready to leave for Africa, the doctor and his wife received confusing messages from the people they knew. Some of their friends questioned their decision: "Are you sure you want to do this?" "What do your kids think?" But others affirmed the choice they had made: "Maybe we should be doing something like this." The couple went ahead with their plans, put their things in storage, and spent a year in a developing country that changed their lives. They left friends and relatives and all that was familiar. But they returned to the United States richer for having given themselves to others in such a unique way.

Now they live in a smaller house and their lifestyle has changed. They have downscaled. They are more aware of the needs of others, and their family has a wealth of memories drawing them closer together. They learned in Africa how hard it is to be caught up in a consumerism mentality when poverty greets you daily at the door. People back home wonder if the doctor was being sued for malpractice—*something* surely must have happened for him and his family to move out of their large home and into a smaller one! Little do they know . . .[8]

NOTES

1. Conversation with a loan officer (November 1992).

2. Steve Advokat, "Paying Down Own Debt May Yield Best Return," *The San Diego Union-Tribune,* 9 November 1992, E1–2.

3. Penelope Wang and Elizabeth Fenner, "How You Can Live Your American Dream," *Money,* November 1992, 171.

4. Marilyn Ross and Tom Ross, *Country Bound!™ Trading Your Business Suit Blues for Blue Jean Dreams* (Buena Vista, Colo.: Communication Creativity, 1992), 254. All quotes from this work are used by permission.

5. Channing Dawson, Editor, "A Few Pretty Good Ideas," *The Practical Homeowner* (May/June 1992), 8.

6. Maxine Hancock, *Living on Less and Liking It More* (Chicago: Moody, 1976), 103.

7. Steve Farrar, *If I'm Not Tarzan and My Wife Isn't Jane, What Are We Doing in the Jungle?* (Portland, Oreg.: Multnomah, 1991), 103–4.

8. Chapel of the Air broadcast; Wheaton, Ill. (9 November 1992).

Jobs
for Sale

PART 3

7

Lateral Downscaling

Daddy' wins out over 'Chief.'" The headline caught our attention. Here was a man who "had it all" and found out that obtaining it wasn't worth the cost. The forty-four-year-old police
chief took a pay cut of $25,000 from his $81,000-a-year salary,
and a demotion to captain, in order to put his family first. Intrigued
by the account, Dave called the chief to find out "the rest of the
story."

Dan (as is the case in the other stories in this book, not his real
name) grew up in the same city of which he was now chief of police.
His desire as a child had been to be a policeman, and he even got to
know several personally as he grew older. In 1971, he married the
daughter of a policeman. Originally he had just wanted to be a patrol-
man, but he started to advance and in 1982 became a lieutenant.

When he was promoted to captain, his personal time evaporated. His job responsibilities overshadowed home interaction. Not
only was he preoccupied with his job when he was home, but his
family times with his children became fewer. As he progressed to
chief, his salary increased, and his time with his family decreased
further. In fact, it became almost nonexistent. Dan was more and
more burdened with police concerns and the politics involved in
holding a public position. On the rare occasions that he did make it
home in time for supper or to see the kids before they went to bed,
work-related phone calls kept him from really enjoying those moments.

While Dan was captain, the police department mandated that policemen must live within the jurisdiction of the city. Since this measure was enacted after Dan became captain, he was permitted to remain where he was living at the time, which was in the suburbs. However, with his promotion to Chief of Police, it became necessary for him to move within the city limits. So Dan and his family leased out their home in the suburbs and rented a second home in the city to comply with the requirement. However, the neighborhood they found suitable for their family was dominated by childless couples, making it a lonely life for their own children.

As their family began growing apart and the tension resulting from an unfavorable community life increased, Dan's wife became more and more dissatisfied with the way they were living. She announced she was taking the kids back to the suburbs. Dan could move with them, or he could rent an apartment in the city and come home on weekends.

At this point an incident occurred that caused Dan to reconsider his ways. A friend, aged fifty, and his wife were both retired and had everything materially they could want. Now they intended to enjoy what they had worked so hard to obtain over many years. But before the couple could fulfill their dreams, the wife died, leaving a husband who felt as though he had nothing in the midst of his plenty. What happened to his friends impressed Dan with the importance of spending time with his family in the present rather than waiting for his retirement years. He decided to move back to the suburbs with his wife.

While Dan was moving up the hierarchy of the police force, he and his wife adhered to roughly the same lifestyle as before. They drove the same cars and were not extravagant with their money. Instead they saved his pay increases. So it was not too difficult financially to let go of the higher salary, since they had not taken themselves to the brink of their earning power. Summing up his motivation for making a decision that doesn't make sense to many, Dan said, "When I finally got it all, I decided it was too much. I preferred the title 'daddy' to 'chief.'"

As a result of Dan's decision to downscale laterally, he was relieved from the political stress of being chief of police and from the requirement of living in the city. At the same time he was freed to pick up the happy life he and his family had built up in the suburbs

and was able to provide intangibles for his children that were lacking in the big city—and he ended up with more time with his family in spite of the commute.[1]

Because of stress and pressure they have had to endure over the last five years, the chiefs of police in forty-one of fifty of the largest cities in the United States have left their positions. For the most part, they felt that too much was expected of them. Instead of just enforcing the law, they were expected to solve root problems and be "miracle workers."[2]

WHY WORK?

Work is a privilege and necessity. We work for the satisfaction of using our skills and abilities. We work to accomplish; to make a difference in our world. We work to bring home a paycheck to provide for our families. We work to alleviate boredom and lack of purpose and replace them with excitement and challenge. We work to escape or to have opportunities to socialize. We work for status, security, or to bolster our self-esteem. We work to gain experience, independence, or control over others. And we work to acquire the material things that we hope will bring us happiness.

Not all of these motivations are healthy. Some will lead us away from the very happiness we seek. Others will cause us to compromise our integrity. Still others will prevent us from gaining maturity through facing the issues we are fleeing.

An even more probing concern deals with the relationship of work and our identity as a person. Can work really define who we are? Work is an extension of who we are, a manifestation of innate characteristics, and a response to need. Work itself is not who we are, but rather exemplifies and illuminates our strengths and weaknesses. Those who have their self-image wrapped up in what they do rather than in who they are are the ones most often devastated by a disability or job loss.

Through our work we can pass on a legacy to our families—not simply by actual accomplishments but in the kind of persons we have become. Work, or lack of it, turns into a stressor when we feel helpless about our situation, are uncertain about the future, experience a continual sense of urgency to produce, and receive little relief from perpetual overwork.

In the recent massive downsizing of corporations (or "rightsizing" as it is sometimes called), the remaining workers often are given added responsibilities that result in increased pressure and time spent on the job. As burnout becomes more progressive and far-reaching, employers will be faced with even greater problems—from lack of efficiency to major blunders costing companies much more than if they had kept the original staff. "If one is under ongoing daily pressure . . . to produce 110 percent, productivity will decline by as much as 25 percent at a cost of more than twenty billion dollars annually," says Richard Fowler in an article in the magazine *Better Life*.[3]

According to a study by the National Institute for Occupational Safety and Health, the people in the top ten most stressful positions are health technicians, waiters and waitresses, licensed practical nurses, quality-control inspectors, musicians, public relations personnel, laboratory technicians, dishwashers, warehouse workers, and nurse's aides.[4]

What this study points to is that not only managers and executives experience pressure on the job, but so also do people holding occupations not readily thought to be stressful. The key factor seems to be the level of control one has over his situation. Less control seems to result in higher stress. When one has more control over his situation, he can take creative steps to alleviate stress. If he has little control, he is likely to experience a sense of helplessness, resulting in greater internal stress.

"Another significant pressure plaguing many of the 99 million men and women in the work force today is the growing threat that advancing technology may automate them out of a job," Tim LaHaye notes in *How to Manage Pressure Before Pressure Manages You.*[5] The fear that your lack of skills may eliminate you from future consideration when your company updates its processes can be a continual stressor.

Internal pressures are added to the external ones. Sometimes internal pressures are harder to deal with because they revolve around the success myth. Consider what two well-known authors have to say about the consequences of buying into that myth: "We are frequently asked if it is possible to 'have it all'—a full and satisfying personal life and a full and satisfying, hard-working professional one. Our answer is: NO. The price of excellence is time, energy, attention and focus, at the very same time that energy, attention and focus could have gone toward enjoying your daughter's soccer game. Excellence is a high cost item."[6] What a sad commentary that so many have forsaken excellence in their family lives for so-called excellence at work. Rather than excellence, it is an unbalanced life —a life only half lived, devoid of intangible and lasting rewards, and often leading to regret in later years.

Another author expounds on the tenets of success as seen in our society today, observing that they include (1) "attaining cultural goals" (as perceived to be important to the specific corporation or community); (2) an elevation in "one's perceived importance" (often a false sense of importance—it's why much of advertising is successful); (3) "an elevation in [one's] power" (along with the authority to control others—as if it really matters in the long run); (4) "an elevation in privilege" (receiving an assigned parking space, a better office, a larger expense account); (5) "an elevation in wealth" (of course that depends on your definition of wealth); and (6) an increase in one's status (an outward confirmation of who we want to be inwardly, but probably aren't).[7]

Yet another author describes the differences between success and significance. Success is centered on self, based on external motivation, oriented toward material things, and concentrated on a changing goal. It revolves around greed, is concerned about immediate rewards, and is focused only on one generation. In contrast, significance is based on concern for others, internal motivation, pursuing stable goals, meeting needs and not wants, achievement with a timeless value, and is multigenerational in scope.[8]

WHAT ARE THE ALTERNATIVES?

The alternatives—with varying degrees of advisability—are to change the number of your working hours, change positions, change companies, change occupations, change your method of working, or, if none of these seems reasonable, change your attitude. Almost any growth requires change. Many people are afraid of change and would rather suffer through an intolerable situation rather than risk the uncertainty of change.

Reducing the Number of Working Hours

The unreasonable demands placed on workers in an effort to save a company actually end up costing more for both the employer and employee. In fact, one source says that it costs the business community "$100 billion a year to cover expenses incurred from stress, including workman's compensation paid as a result; sick days; and worker inefficiency. Even at that figures are thought to be on the low side."[9]

If you are putting in enough hours overtime to make you feel as though you work one-and-a-half or two full-time jobs, then maybe it's necessary to consider just how feasible it is for you to continue doing as you are. This is even more true if in addition to working long hours, you have a significant commute, making the strain even greater.

When you *are* at home physically, are you in tune with your family emotionally or is your house just a place to let the frustrations from work smolder while you plop in front of the television set? And what about your health? Are you fatigued lately, or rundown? Do you lack motivation? Do you catch colds more frequently? Or are you easily irritated, grumpy, and miserable to be around?

Are your kids becoming more difficult to handle, but you have neither the time nor the inclination to deal with them? And what about your marriage? Has it, too, deteriorated in the past few months? Have you lost your zest for living and find yourself just trying to endure one more day? Although many of us will go through bouts with various crises in our lifetime, living in a state of continual crisis is beyond the ability of most people.

In order to extradite yourself from this no-win situation, sit down and examine your work schedule. It is helpful to do this exercise on a piece of paper because the numbers can often shake us up when we have allowed smoke screens to shield us from reality. Over the past few months, what was the average total number of hours per week that you worked? How many hours a week do you spend commuting? Or doing work from home? If that total figure is greater than sixty hours a week, including commuting time, your life may be out of balance. Until you take measures to bring it back into balance, all of life for you will be off-kilter.

Maybe you began by working an extra hour or two in the evening "just to finish up" before coming home. Next that became the norm. After that you began to bring extra work home "to try to get ahead before the next day's onslaught." That intention then spilled over into the weekend. But lately when you bring work home you find yourself avoiding it at all costs. Your creativity has been stifled and you feel stagnant. Even though you avoid the work you bring home, it is still hanging over your head, preventing you from enjoying what little time you do have with your family.

You may have started to resent the feeling of never being caught up, and your frustration comes out easily against your family. They are walking on eggs trying not to aggravate your nerves. You're just not fun to be around anymore. The kids avoid you and your spouse tries to have other plans when he or she thinks you will be around. It has come to the point where you even resent going to work at all. Your job is no longer enjoyable, you feel as though you are wasting your life, and the demands and wants of your family linger in your mind as you contemplate chucking the whole thing.

One corporate worker hated his job so much "he'd drive a few extra blocks to delay going into the office. Today, he runs a $1.75 million pipeline company from his spare bedroom."[10]

Companies that have reduced employee benefits, changed hands through a merger or sell-out, demanded substantial overtime, or decreased their staff have the highest incidents of burnout, according to a survey conducted for Northwestern National Life Insurance

Company. Furthermore, one-third of American workers thought about quitting their jobs last year due to work-related stress.

The next step is to write up a one- or two-page proposal to be given to your supervisor. It should include your actual working hours for the last few months. Using the statistics given earlier, mention the premise that after a certain point heavy work schedules typically reduce efficiency more than is gained by working overtime.

Suggest ways you would like to begin cutting back. For example, if you currently work 70 hours a week and you want to cut back, perhaps shaving two to three hours off a day may be the place to start. Or maybe not working at all on Saturday or Sunday would help alleviate the strain of working longer hours during the week. If you don't seek an alternative before your health gives out, you will be forced to accept a less desirous one later.

Decrease in Responsibilities

Corporate downsizing, an unclear job description, a supervisor reducing *his* workload, or a company's finding it easier to give an on-site employee more work than it is to hire an additional person are all reasons people feel burdened by too many responsibilities. If this is true for you, perhaps your family priorities have taken second place to work and you feel as though you are being asked to do what is beyond reason. In that case, it is a good idea to prepare another proposal similar to the one given above, but this one focused on suggestions for reducing your work hours. In addition, you should make a list of your specific tasks with their corresponding time commitment.

By evaluating exactly how you spend your time, your employer may decide certain tasks are not worth doing. Or your employer may decide that what was at one time perceived as being a high priority item is really an outdated task that was a pet project of an ex-manager. Whatever the outcome, if you make such a list you will be more attuned to what you are trying to accomplish, your boss will be impressed with your resourcefulness, and you will feel more in control of what is expected of you. While you are at it, write out your ideal job description. Explain to your supervisor what you feel your strengths are and why it would benefit the company to allow you to focus more on those areas.

In exchange for a decrease either in your working hours or your responsibilities, be willing to negotiate a reduced salary or benefit package. You may suggest that you and the company put the new schedule into practice on a temporary basis. Sometimes a company is hesitant to make a change because it doesn't want to be locked into a permanent arrangement. But if you set up a new working relationship with your company on a temporary basis, it will give your boss the opportunity to see your increased enthusiasm and productivity on the job, and he may be more willing to make it a permanent change.

"Your employer will be more receptive to making a change if you enact a campaign on behalf of the company a month or two before presenting your request. This entails thinking of creative ways to save the company money, doing your job conscientiously, being a positive influence in the work environment, and overall making yourself a valuable employee, keeping in mind the ultimate needs and goals of the company and how you can best meet them."[11]

In the meantime, determine that you will set aside two to three evenings a week when you will not bring work home. Rest and recharge and renew. Rest from your constant mental and physical preoccupation with work. Recharge your inspiration for living. Renew your ties with your family. Enjoy yourself outside of work, and you will probably be more productive while on the job.

One well-known insurance company suggests approaching the supervisor and explaining the dynamics behind your request. In this way you can put your career on hold without damaging future advancement. Then, later, when you *are* ready to advance, let them know.

Dave interviewed an executive from a Midwestern company, asking what would be the best approach for a similar request of their corporation. The response was that company personnel are not power driven but rather are very casual. Executives go to work in blue jeans. The executive believed that atmosphere lent itself to a more relaxed and less stressful work environment.

During a session of a six-week series on downscaling, we asked the participants for feedback on major changes that had occurred in their work in the last two years, and what would they would change if they could. Here are some of their responses:

- "As an educator, my role is constantly being changed. I am being expected to be Mom, Dad, referee, counselor, psychologist, etc. The demands on teachers are overwhelming —all these roles plus trying to help children learn skills they need to 'survive' and be successful."

- "Our plant has undergone major changes, cutting back on personnel and putting greater work loads on the people left here, making us feel guilty if we aren't willing to work the overtime. It's frustrating because they never tell us ahead of time what our work schedule will be. I would like more communication."

- "We have had a lot more overtime, plus more responsibilities have been placed on me. It has taken a lot of time away from our family. There is more arguing within our family. Changes I would like: Hire more workers as a second shift, be able to take breaks and lunches, slow the pace down."

- "I went from shift work to straight days. It gave me more available time with family and reduced [the number of] hours [I had to work on] the weekend. I would like a work station in the home, and less stress."

- "I have more paperwork and less time to teach and plan. More hassles at work are probably mirrored by more stress at home."

- "A cutback in staff resulted in work overload. Extra stress! Additional responsibilities. This sometimes adds tension at home because I'm tired. I would like to quit and work at home."

- "There was a cut in staff, complete change in performance. More hours, cannot keep up. Lots of anxiety because there is not enough time to complete tasks, and if I attempt to give more to my family I feel I am neglecting the job. Would like them to hire more staff and slow the pace."

- "I have taken an administrative position with added responsibilities. Greater number of people to supervise. Additional responsibility that I was not supposed to have. Benefits: I make the decisions with staff input, more money, enjoy working with children and adults. Detrimental aspects: less family time. I would like less paperwork, [more] appreciation for what I do, expectation that work ends at 4:30 P.M. (the day begins at 7:15 A.M.)."

Should you consider a change? Are you unhappy at work most of the time? Are you learning new things, or are you stagnating? Do you enjoy your work environment, the people, the work, the location, the pay, the benefits, and the schedule? Granted, it is difficult to find the "perfect" position. In fact, in lean times, to be working at all is a powerful incentive to put up with the drawbacks in a particular position. But, for the long haul, if you dislike many things about your job *and* it is keeping you from developing closer relationships at home, then it may be wise to begin looking for another position while you are still employed. The purpose is to find employment that will lessen time and energy demands on you.

After twelve years as the CEO of Alaska Airlines, Bruce Kennedy, 52, gave up his position in order to devote more time to serving others. Kennedy received *Aviation Week and Space Technology*'s top-ranking Laurels Award in 1990. During his time with Alaska Airlines, the company's revenues

> grew from less than $100 million to more than $1 billion. . . . In that span of years, he helped transform a demoralized and virtually bankrupt company into one that has been repeatedly honored as the best airline in the United States and one of the best in the world. The *Anchorage Times* wrote, "It is an uncommon event when a highly successful business leader renounces life at the very highest executive level in favor of a new career in simple service to others. That's what Bruce R. Kennedy is doing, in a move that might astonish those who don't know this particular airline chief.
>
> "But Bruce Kennedy is an uncommon man. And it was quite in keeping with his deep religious conviction and his humble quiet character that he would decide there is more to life than a big salary and all the perks that go with being the Chief Executive Officer of one of the world's most acclaimed aviation companies."[12]

Touché!

NOTES

1. Conversation with chief of police. Used by permission.
2. CBS, "Sunday Evening News," 25 October 1992.
3. Richard Fowler, "The Price of Success," *Better Life* 1 no. 4 (Summer 1992), 90.
4. Keith W. Sehnert, M.D., *Stress/Unstress* (Minneapolis: Augsburg, 1981), 38–39.

5. Tim LaHaye, *How to Manage Pressure Before Pressure Manages You* (Grand Rapids: Zondervan, 1983), 46.

6. Thomas J. Peters and Nancy K. Austin, *A Passion for Excellence: The Leadership Difference* (New York: Random, 1985), 117.

7. Steve Farrar, *If I'm Not Tarzan and My Wife Isn't Jane, What Are We Doing in the Jungle?* (Portland, Oreg.: Multnomah, 1991), 39–44.

8. Charles Bradshaw and Dave Gilbert, *Too Hurried to Love: Creating a Lifestyle for Lasting Relationships* (Eugene, Oreg.: Harvest, 1991), 67.

9. Donald T. DeCarlo, Sr., vice president of Commercial Insurance Resources, quoted in *Secrets of Executive Success,* by Mark Golin, Mark Bricklin, and David Diamond (Emmaus, Pa.: Rodale, 1991), 414.

10. Janean Huber, "Free at Last," *Entrepreneur* 20, no.9 (September 1992), 101.

11. Kathy Babbitt, "Lateral Downscaling," *Downscaling 46510,* October 1992, 5.

12. "MAF Profile; Bruce R. Kennedy, Chairman of the Board, MAF-US," *Flight Log* [Mission Aviation Fellowship] 6, no. 10 (October 1992), 5.

8

Working Alternatives for Today's Lifestyles

How would you like to get up in the morning, don comfortable clothes, eat a relaxed breakfast, have meaningful family interaction, send the kids off to school knowing they are loved, and then not have to jump in your car for a hectic, stress-filled commute? Or throughout the day not to have to deal with minor, frustrating interruptions, boring meetings, unproductive chats, busywork, and unnecessary phone calls? Or, if your child is sick, not to have to deal with anxiety from missing another day of work? Or not to run up your credit cards for a wide selection of office apparel, lunches out, day-care, gas, parking and tolls, and office donations and gifts?

And what about your work itself? Wouldn't you like to be more productive and challenged, make fewer mistakes, enjoy a less pressure-filled setting with more flexibility and freedom? And, to top it off, to know that you are helping control traffic and pollution? Do you think your employer would appreciate savings on office space, utilities, and other overhead and have you become 20 percent more productive for his benefit?

Then take heart. There may be a way for you to have the "best of both worlds"—a steady income and more independence. The growing phenomenon that embraces all these characteristics is telecommuting. Fueling this trend is the affordability of the personal computer, stricter environmental guidelines for businesses with one hundred employees or more, increasing costs of overhead to maintain workers in an office setting, and the need for corporations to retain or attract qualified personnel by offering a home-working option.

In an article in *Compute!* Rosalind Resnick says: "With the recession forcing companies to pinch every penny, more and more managers recognize that there are sizable bottom-line benefits to letting employees work from home. Not only are telecommuters happier and more productive, studies show, but having fewer workers at the office or production plant means reduced expenses and overhead."[1]

When we talk about telecommuting, we are referring to the transfer of information electronically for the purpose of connecting a worker with an employer. This is facilitated through the use of computers, modems, and fax machines. It often involves the employee's working at home for the most part, with infrequently scheduled appearances at the job site or a satellite office.

Telecommuting is gaining in favor throughout the country. "In the last four years the number of telecommuters in the U.S. has doubled to more than 6 million."[2] Telecommuting has become "the fastest-growing segment of the U.S. work-at-home trend."[3]

"Fortunately," one executive notes, "more U.S. companies are finally realizing that domestic peace and worker productivity are closely linked and are therefore offering part-time positions, telecommuting options and job sharing, which information systems workers are increasingly taking advantage of. 'To a great extent, having productive people on the job is a function of keeping their family happiness intact'"[4]

Telecommuting is also an alternative on the horizon for the up-and-coming generation. Since employers in the future will be drawing from a smaller pool of skilled workers, and since there is a greater corporate understanding of the importance of families, today's young people hope "for longer vacations, greater parental leaves, more flexible working conditions. . . . Many college students, while nervous about their economic prospects, are equally wary of the fast lane. . . . The *Time* poll found that 51% put having a long and happy marriage and raising well-adjusted children ahead of career success (29%)."[5]

President George Bush, in a May 1991 letter to the Minnesota Telecommuting Conference, endorsed telecommuting as a solution to several societal problems we face today.

Telecommuting is a concept that is emerging from the grass roots of America, and its time has come. Across the Nation, both employers and employees are recognizing the many benefits of telecommuting. If even a small segment of our work force spent one or two days a week working from home or from a satellite work center, we would not only save immense amounts of time and gasoline, but also enjoy a significant reduction in traffic congestion and in air pollution.

Most important, perhaps, telecommuting benefits families as well as business. In today's changing labor force, telecommuting helps to meet the needs of working parents. It fosters productivity and improves morale by allowing parents to work closer to the people that they're really working for: their children.

Telecommuting is a promising choice for the future—one that is being embraced across the Nation because it presents workers and employers with welcome alternatives to traditional job settings. As American commerce moves into the future, we should remember that sometimes the best policy is not moving people, but moving their work.[6]

The potential benefit for the environment can be tremendous. "If only 5 percent of commuters in Los Angeles County telecommuted only one day each week," 47,000 fewer tons of pollution would be spewed into the atmosphere, saving 9.5 million gallons of gasoline a year.[7]

In corporate shake-ups, personnel are reorganized and shuffled in an effort to increase the bottom line. Telecommuting is sometimes a way to streamline a company's employment picture. "As companies decentralize and reform themselves around their information networks—tying branch offices, telecommuting employees and customers together with private networks, satellites, laptop computers and fax machines—the result is sometimes the end of entire middle layers of management."[8]

The magazine *Home Office Computing* surveyed over 100 Fortune 1000 companies and government organizations and found that "America is on its way to realizing the dreams of uncrowded highways, cleaner air, and happier, more productive employees."[9] Among the reasons given for increasing telecommuting in the future are that it increases employee retention, decreases traffic and pollution liabilities, eases home and workplace conflicts, decreases office overhead, and contains at the potential for an increase in productivity.

The ability to work independently is the key ingredient for allowing an employee to work from home, according to this same survey. The main reason companies hesitate implementing telecommuting options is management resistance and fear of loss of control over their employees. Yet where telecommuting has actually been put into place, 89 percent of telecommuters are reported to be very satisfied with the arrangement, with 11 percent being somewhat satisfied, and 0 percent being dissatisfied.[10]

IS TELECOMMUTING RIGHT FOR YOU?

In evaluating the telecommuting option determine if you are ready to give up the corporate environment of busyness for one of isolation at home. Do you have the motivation and self-discipline to carry out your work? Managers are often far ahead in developing the qualities of a good telecommuter: he should be familiar with the tenets of efficient time management, self-motivated and able to work well on his own, understand the larger scope of a project or proposal, and have had a taste of independence and found it palatable.

Many consider telecommuting an answer to job dissatisfaction. Maybe they are working at their current position because of money, prestige, or pressure from parents or spouse and want out of the daily hassle. They may be overworked, underchallenged, tired of the smoke, noise, and sometimes a lack of ethics in the office place. Telecommuting may offer what they are looking for. At the same time people need to be aware of the drawbacks. Amy Bellinger and Helen

La Van, in an article in *Home Office Commuting,* warn that "a laid-back, family-oriented company is not likely to pay as well . . . . Workers looking for new jobs must understand the trade-offs and prioritize what is important to them . . . because you don't get it all."[11]

Implementing a telecommuting position can help you guard against unemployment by putting certain factors in place while you are still employed. Getting set up in a home office enables you to get used to being on your own, working independently, managing tasks that would be similar to running a business, and getting a workspace into place for starting a side business through your home office. In the meantime you could be upgrading your training, skills, and knowledge while becoming proficient in an area of business should you lose your current employment. "The telecommuting trailblazers for the most part have been independent business people who seize the chance to shed the armor of a road warrior for the relative informality and calm of small-town life."[12]

It may be more advantageous to seek telecommuting options within your own company than to apply with a different firm that already has a telecommuting program. Talk to others who have been instrumental in establishing a precedent for telecommuting in their company. Find out how they did it, the areas of resistance, and how they were overcome. Inquire also about the benefits and drawbacks of actually carrying out the program.

What things hold you to the office? Can they be handled in such a way so as to make working at home possible? Think through creative alternatives. For instance, if you are fearful that your absence will cause you to lose ground in terms of advancement, create ways to be more visible than in the past. Hand in attractive, well-organized weekly or bi-weekly updates on your activities and accomplishments. Make sure your work is measurable in some way and can be translated to home projects. Garner publicity for your accomplishments, both inside and outside the corporate structure. Add these to your communication packets. Show tangible results, and your boss won't be as concerned about your physical absence.

Consider also what parts of a project can best be handled from home. One author writes about dividing projects into three phases: preparation, production, and presentation. In the preparation stage a worker plans, interviews, and lays the groundwork for the production phase. During the second stage, the worker actually carries out the project and may benefit from the quiet atmosphere of a home office. Often home-workers access the company's computer system at night when demand and usage cost are lower. The presentation phase allows the worker to introduce what he produced during the production stage to a supervisor or client. [13]

One organization gives workers "personal computers to work on from home doing application development, allowing full-time workers to reduce their hours so they can spend more time with their young children and allowing some workers to move into less demanding jobs where they will not need to put in extra hours on a regular basis."[14]

There are positives and negatives to approaching your employer if you sense change is in the air for your company. There is potential for a negative result and possibly even job loss when an economic downturn is occurring in your region or industry; if the company you work for has large corporate debt and little cash flow; if your employer has put a hold on hiring, promotions, or bonuses; there is talk of mergers, buy outs, or a move to a less expensive location; cut-backs are taking place in every area; and management personnel are being dismissed or asked to take early retirement.

On the positive side, you can save the company money by telecommuting and you will be more productive. On the negative side, your application to work on a telecommuting basis might give management an excuse to claim you are dissatisfied with your job and consequently provide your supervisor with an easy out if he is already being forced to reduce his operating budget. Or your supervisor may react negatively to your proposal because it gives him the sense of not being fully in control and thus may make him or her feel threatened.

Here are some pointers to help you surmount the hurdle of approaching your boss, should you decide to "go for it."

- Work out a budget proposal indicating the actual dollar savings and other benefits to your employer.
- Outline how you will spend your time, what you hope to accomplish, and include a hypothetical weekly progress report.
- Give assurance that you will be readily available to customers or other office personnel by phone, fax, or modem; that you will attend scheduled meetings; that you are willing to try the

arrangement on a temporary basis; and that you have a track record of working well without supervision.

- If you are not familiar with the latest technology, take classes to upgrade your skills.
- Network with others who have been successful at telecommuting.

Sears Roebuck and Company recently moved its headquarters from its downtown Chicago tower to the suburbs of Hoffman Estates, thirty-five miles west. They uprooted five thousand jobs and in the process expanded their telecommuting department. According to an interview Dave had with a representative of human resources at Sears, in order to avoid losing a number of their key employees as a result of the move, the company allowed people in the data processing systems area to telecommute if they wanted. The company provided all the equipment the employees needed. Sears discovered that productivity increased and the employees enjoyed savings in clothing and travel expenses and better family times.

Before the move, management was concerned about being able to supervise workers, and employees wanted to know if their careers would suffer because they were out of sight. The drawback for the company was the expense of setting up home offices at the same time it was implementing the move to the suburbs—and in a recession. (We surmise that the company will recoup its economic outlay in reduced overhead at the job site.) Sears is also concerned that employees will overwork themselves when their equipment is so readily accessible. Perhaps employees won't know when to quit. The company wants its employees to have a healthy family life and to avoid burnout. After all, these are valuable workers, and Sears wants to keep them for a long time.[15]

It is amazing what kind of work can be done from home with the availability of modern technology. Ophthalmologist John Garden of Lexington, Kentucky, examines his patients' eyes long-distance from a computer screen in his office while saving the government money. Some of his patients are federal prisoners. In the past the Bureau of Prisons needed to fund the services of two guards plus transportation costs in addition to the actual eye exam. With a computer, modem, and videocamera set up in an examination room five miles away at the federal penitentiary, the cost has been reduced from $220 per patient to $40.[16]

A company called Global Telematics helps small companies start using telecommuting as a viable option within their business. The president of the company is John S. Niles, 322 N.W. 74th Street, Seattle, WA 98117-4931; telephone 206-781-9493.

CASE HISTORY

An editorial director for a large publishing house has been telecommuting for about a year-and-a-half. Here's his story:

> In terms of my background, I had my own business and I know the ins and outs of a home business. It matches my comfort level. You can't automatically assume that because you work at home part of the time, you are the kind of person who can concentrate and have discipline in the midst of distraction. Even if you have a home office, there are still distractions from other family members.
>
> A lot of people will not be cut out for it even in a proper working environment. I redid my entire basement. It's a large office. I think it is more important with an office at home to have room to move around and work in. I have adequate lighting and heating. A proper environment includes a fax machine that allows me to stay in touch with the office. Voice mail is even better and more convenient and efficient for both parties, not just one party. I tend to do my voice mail both at the beginning and the end of the day. The fax machine was donated to us. The company pays for paper and the telephone bill. I have a card with a code so I don't have to go through the hassle of sending them bills and figure out what is theirs and mine.
>
> I am a manager and an editorial director. I have a manager under me on a daily basis to make sure the schedule is in shape. When I am in the office I have a lot of meetings I have to go to. For six or eight months I went into work five days a week. The commuting time was down time and created fatigue when I was in the office. As acquisitions editor I spend time with authors in person and on the phone. I do a lot of reading. When I am in the office I need personal contact with editors, have editorial meetings, and must interface with marketing and publishers. My reading time was being absorbed and suffered after a long day of commuting. As a result, I had to finish up on my own time.
>
> So we agreed to try [telecommuting] two days a week to review manuscripts and talk to authors [from my home office]. The other three days—Mondays, Wednesdays, and Fridays—I would have nothing but meetings. I am a lot more productive, no doubt about it. I have been doing this over a year-and-a-half and I think I have only had a handful of

days where I have had to cut back to working at home one day a week. Some weeks I actually spend three days a week at home.

I think I am disciplined enough that I definitely try to make sure in the evenings I spend time with my family. There are times when I have worked in the evenings. I might lose an hour or two during a workday, but I can make that up in the evening.

There's always the chance of miscommunication. I tell my employees, "You don't always have to use my voice mail. You can call me live at home." Communication with more than one party when you are in the office is easier. You talk to one person, then you can go to another desk and talk to someone else to relay a bit of information. That process is more difficult working at home. The other thing that can happen, especially if one or more people have a home office, is sometimes just plain miscommunication.

Fortunately I only have to respond to my publisher. I send him a monthly report, voice mail every day where a matter pertains to him, and meet over the phone. We can cover a lot on the phone in an hour.[17]

All in all, this telecommuter has found the arrangement conducive to fostering a more enjoyable work situation as well as developing closer family relationships.

OTHER ALTERNATIVES

Cutting Back to One Income

Many families are in a position to make it on one income if they alter their standard of living. In the process of providing material "things" for our families, we are losing them to pseudofamilies in the form of gangs, destructive peer groups, or cults. Teenage suicide is rampant. Since 1950, the suicide rate among teens has escalated by 300 percent.[18] One source reports that research shows that "stronger families and stronger faith are the two great deterrents to suicide among youth."[19] Are we listening? Listening to the cries of a hurting generation with parents too busy to care, too worn out to bother, or too engrossed in their work to hear? In *More to Life Than Having It All* Bob Welch says: "The point is painfully clear: Many of us seem unwilling to give up luxury items for ourselves in exchange for necessary time with our children. The question isn't, 'Can we afford to live on less?' but 'Are we willing to live on less?'"[20]

One mother made the choice to put her family before a job. "I worked as a part-time OB nurse at the local community hospital. I have three children ages 10, 8, and 5. My husband has a management position in a local orthopedic company and travels often. Working every other weekend was eating into our family time, trying to juggle my husband's travel schedule with my work schedule, with the kids' school schedules and juggling and juggling. . . . It was taking a toll on me and my family. I miss working. I really enjoyed it, but things are more relaxed at home. My husband's travel is easier for both of us now that I don't have to juggle schedules. I worked for the extras and my spending cash. I miss it, but I enjoy being home and greeting my kids with milk and cookies after school. I have been blessed and I am thankful I have the option not to work."

Part-time

If you are in a two-income family you have more leeway in your working alternatives, particularly if you want to cut back to regular part-time hours. With today's hectic lifestyles, it is especially helpful if at least one of the couple does not have to work full-time. Balance is easier to maintain in a home where adequate time is given for household tasks and preparing healthy meals. As a result, all family members benefit.

One working mother and wife cut back her hours to part-time and found the advantages more than made up for the decrease in her paycheck.

> How important is it for your kids to have you home? Our children are 19, 17, and 15. They said, "Yes, we want you home and we are willing to do with less." The whole family must get caught up in the trend of a downscaled lifestyle or else it will be: "It's great, Mom's not working and is giving us brownies after school! Can I have $70 for a new outfit?"
>
> It's important to my kids that I get to as many of their events as I can. We're a talking family. We talk about important things happening in their lives, what makes them sad, about their friendships, about sex. It's wonderful! But, when I'm busy, and running around, and grumpy, they just don't talk. They go off and watch TV, or go [out] with friends instead.
>
> When I'm not working, or when I work part-time, the house is more comfortable and peaceful, and there is not as much bickering. I have time to be more economical, especially for meals. I don't need as many nice clothes. We do more entertaining. We rent videos and have popcorn instead of going to movies. We read more and play games, take bike rides and go to the beach.
>
> We have more time to have fun and to know who our children are. We have more input into their personalities, and can listen when they are

hurting. That to me is the most important part of being home. I can be attuned to signs of children in trouble, struggling, or hurting. When your kids are 12 to 19, they need you just as much as in their younger years.

A lot of making it on a downscaled lifestyle has to do with your book on self-discipline. You have to discipline yourself to use your time wisely, to get along with less [and not] spend money. Downscaling has a whole lot more to do with your attitude than your lifestyle. It doesn't mean going without things; it means investing in relationships. [21]

Well said!

One of the women attending our downscaling series wrote,

I resigned from a teaching position after developing the program for 14 years. It just got too big—little to no help from administration—I just couldn't do it all! My son needed to repeat a grade and after having him tested we learned he has some learning disabilities. He needed my help *now* and there just was no extra time. Now I work as an office manager for a counseling service. I teach one night a week (college courses). We have less income—we do fewer things and *plan* those that we do. There is more "pressure" on my husband financially. I don't have summers "off." I have a "dead-end" current job and I miss the intellectual stimulation, a way to receive praise, advance in my work and grow to use my training and talents. On the positive side, we have study time, all of my children are doing well in school, the chest pains are gone and I sleep well.

Rather than looking for a different part-time position, try working out an arrangement with your current employer to cut back your hours. It will save the expense of finding and training a replacement for you. For additional suggestions in this area, contact the Association of Part-Time Professionals, a national organization promoting flexible work options (Crescent Plaza, Suite 216, 7700 Leesburg Pike, Falls Church, VA 22043; 703-734-7975). Their goal is to assist professionals in pursuing alternative work schedules, provide up-to-date information of interest to this group, and serve as a networking organization. We are currently reviewing their "Part-Timer's Resource Kit," which offers practical information if you are considering this option (cost: $7.00, which includes postage). There may also be books available at your local library or through the inter-library loan system. If you live near a college, you can often use their library without a fee unless you want to check out resources.

Job Sharing

Job sharing occurs when two people divide a full-time job into two equal or unequal work schedules. Most often the division is twenty hours per worker, but individual employees can usually arrange a varied schedule. One worker may work every morning and the other every afternoon. Or the schedule may involve one employee working Mondays, Wednesdays, and Fridays while the other works Tuesdays and Thursdays. For job sharing to work there must be good communication between the two workers. They need to develop flowcharts of their work and set up frequent meetings.

There are benefits to employers in setting up job-sharing arrangements.

1. They enable employers to retain valuable employees. During times of crisis or life transition employees may want or need to cut back on their working hours. It is often more beneficial to keep a valued employee on part-time status than to search for and train a new worker. The current worker would then be responsible for hiring and training his or her job-sharing partner.
2. Usually there is greater base of skill and talent when two workers share a work slot. The employer benefits from the strengths of each. The employees will be using their "up time" for work, saving the company money through lack of efficiency in the employee's "down time." More actual work will be accomplished, enthusiasm will remain high for the job, and creativity will be multiplied.
3. There is a reduction in absenteeism and vacancies because of vacation time. The position will be filled even if one worker has sick children or goes on a trip.

There are also drawbacks to job sharing from an employer's point of view.

1. The employer might not fully understand the concept of job sharing.
2. There will be a slight increase in bookkeeping.

3. Depending on what benefits are offered, job sharing may be more expensive for the company (although the increase in productivity should balance out this negative).[22]

It is important for job sharers to be compatible, flexible, organized, and dedicated to collaboration, communication, and commitment.

Flextime

Flextime allows workers to have more freedom in scheduling their days. For instance, if an employee needs to be at home with his children until they leave for school, it would be advantageous for him to begin his workday at 9 A.M. instead of 8 A.M. To compensate, he might work until 6 P.M. instead of leaving at 5 P.M. His spouse could then arrange to be home in the afternoon so that their children would not fall into the proverbial "latch-key syndrome." Some programs entail allowing employees to work three or four long days and then be off the other one or two days of the normal work week.

In an article on flextime Karen Lavine observes: "Management sees [flextime] as a low-cost way to enhance productivity, facilitate recruitment, improve worker morale, and reduce absenteeism, overtime, tardiness, and job turnover. Workers see that it can make juggling work and family a far less arduous task."[23]

Most flextime schedules require workers to be on the job during a core period of several hours when interaction between employees is at its height. This option has traditionally lowered absenteeism and attrition rates. It allows for a sense of community among employees and yet gives them a sense of freedom, which results in greater enthusiasm for their jobs and hence greater productivity for the company.

One danger of a company's decreasing the work hours of its employees or changing the work schedule is the potential for employees to overwork to offset the negatives of a shorter work week. One man said, "My hours and pay have been cut back. The hours have also been rearranged so that on days I'm at work I don't see my family. [On those days the company expects him to put in a twelve-hour day.] The only benefit [to the program is that] I have three, sometimes four days out of there, and those days I would have had with the family. But because of the cut in pay, I took on selling insurance."

Phased Retirement

By gradually reducing a valued employee's working hours, an employer can retain experience and skill often lacking in newer employees. Rather than stopping his work abruptly when he retires, the veteran employee could be using the last months of his career training his younger counterpart. Both the worker and the company would benefit from such a program, and its success would increase morale and lead to more positive public relations.

FINDING JOBS THAT ALLOW
FOR CREATIVE WORK ALTERNATIVES

If you are currently looking for a job that offers greater alternatives, consider what one source found in the success rate of various job search avenues: networking, 63 percent; employment agencies and search firms, 13 percent; classified ads, 11 percent; other (computer job banks, trade-association postings), 11 percent; and blanket mailings, 2 percent.[24] Today there are more than thirty thousand kinds of jobs. An organization called Career Pathways (P.O. Box 1476, Gainesville, GA 30503-1476l; telephone 1-800-722-1976) can help you narrow the field and choose a fulfilling career. The company offers career guidance assessment, feedback, and resource materials with an emphasis on stewardship of "talents, . . . gifts, abilities, and personal style of work. The Career Pathways program is based on the biblical teaching that God has a purpose for each individual and has [given each of us the gifts we need] to fulfill that purpose or calling. Our purpose is fulfilled in a large way through our life work which we call our occupation, career or profession."[25]

NOTES

1. Rosalind Resnick, "Remote Possibilities," *Compute!* 13, no. 10 (October 1991), 78, 80.
2. David C. Churbuck and Jeffrey S. Young, "The Virtual Workplace," *Forbes,* 23 November 1992, 186.

3. "The 10-Second Commute," *Home Office Computing* 9, no. 12 (December 1991), 45 (quoting Thomas E. Miller, vice president of Home Office Research at Link Resources).

4. Alan J. Ryan, "Struggling with Juggling *Is* Career and Family Life," *Computerworld*, November 19, 1990, 112 (quoting James C. Miller, vice president of information technology at James River Corporation of Virginia in Richmond, Virginia).

5. Ann Blackman (Washington), Elizabeth Taylor (Chicago), Jane Willwerth (Los Angeles), "The Road to Equality," *Time* 136, no. 19 (Fall 1990, special issue), 13.

6. President George Bush in a letter to the Minnesota Telecommuting Conference, May 1991. Printed in *Home Office Computing* 10, no. 2 (February 1992), 45.

7. Marilyn Ross and Tom Ross, *Country Bound!*™ *Trade Your Business Suit Blues for Blue Jean Dreams* (Buena Vista, Colo.: Communication Creativity, 1992), 282. All quotes from this work are used by permission.

8. Churbuck and Young, 186.

9. Amy Bellinger and Helen La Van, "Telecommuting: Has Its Time Come?" *Home Office Computing* 11, no. 12 (December 1992), 50.

10. Ibid., 52, 54.

11. Ryan, 112.

12. Leah Beth Ward, "The Mixed Blessings of Telecommuting," *The New York Times*, September 20, 1992.

13. Brad Schepp, "The Best Opportunities for Telecommuters," *Home Office Computing* 8, no. 10 (October 1990), 50.

14. Ryan, 112.

15. Personal interview; also Churbuck and Young, 187.

16. Churbuck and Young, 187.

17. Personal interview with the editorial director of a large publishing house, 9 December 1992.

18. Dan Coats, "America's Youth: A Crisis of Character," *American Family Association Journal*, November/December 1991, 18.

19. Family Research Council, *Free to Be Family* (Washington, D.C.: 1992), 88.

20. Bob Welch, *More to Life Than Having It All: Living a Life You Won't Regret* (Eugene, Oreg.: Harvest, 1991), 137.

21. "Letter of the Month," *Downscaling 46510*, July 1992, 6.

22. See Jan Easter Bahls, "Getting Full-Time Work from Part-Time Employees," *Management Review* 79 (February 1990), 50–52.

23. Karen Lavine, "Flextime—It works!" *Parents* 65, no. 9 (September 1990), 170.

24. Source: Drake Beam Morin, in "Good News, You're Fired!" by Michael J. Wiess, *Redbook*, July 1992, 72.

25. Career Pathways Application, 4.

9

The Grass Roots Trend That Is Changing America

For many, lateral downscaling, job sharing, and flextime are not sufficient working alternatives to provide them with the freedom, control, flexibility, and financial opportunities they are seeking. As a result, they are turning to the alternative of establishing and operating a home business. Author and futurist Rowan Wakefield of Deer Isle, Maine, predicts that there may be as many as 40 million home-run enterprises by the year 2000.[1]

As increasing numbers of women entered the work force over the last two decades, more and more found that owning their own businesses provided a better alternative to punching a time clock. Although the statement below depicts career potential as a fundamental reason for starting a business (it is from an advertisement for product distributors), in reality women are looking for more than just financial gain. "The Department of Labor reports that many working women are leaving the fast track and opting for part-time employment to gain more time with family. Yet for career-driven women, part-time and flextime don't offer strong advancement opportunities. As a result, the U.S. Small Business Administration reports that women-owned businesses are the fastest growing segment of the small business community."[2]

Many of the reasons for starting a home-based business are the same for both sexes. Men and women alike want to have more time to be with the family and maintain a healthy lifestyle. Both enjoy a more comfortable and informal work setting. Both can save money on gas, meals out, child care, office attire, and overhead. Both desire more control over their lives and less routine and more flexibility. Both dislike the long commute to work. Both want to make a difference in the world. Or, as is becoming quite common, both lost their jobs.

A survey in the November 1990 issue of *Home Office Computing* magazine revealed factors true of people who work from home. They can better balance family and career (90 percent); their children are happy to have them work at home (85 percent); they feel they are better parents (84 percent); their children better understand and appreciate their work (81 percent); their children are more likely to be entrepreneurial adults (81 percent); their children are less likely to use drugs or alcohol (76 percent); and they are more involved with their children's school activities (72 percent).[3]

Not only are women starting businesses in record numbers, but older Americans (older than us, but not so old) are taking the plunge as well.

> It was once unusual for people over 50 to launch a new business. Today this daring mid-life venture is played out in every state in the union. The Roper Organization forecasts the next major wave of entrepreneurs will include an unusually high proportion of older Americans. Many of these people have been forced out of jobs by early retirement. Close to 20 percent of start-ups are begun by men and women age 50 or over. Folks in their sixties and seventies are retiring from one career, then starting in an entirely new field—finally doing what they've dreamed of all their lives.[4]

Yet another segment striking out on their own is made up of those who want to escape the system; those who are looking at the next rung and wondering if what's at the top is only a farce; those who seem to have everything going for them—along with millions of others who are eager to snuff them out of the competition for that next promotion. "They're fed up, tired of relocating, scared or laid-off. And they're not going to take corporate America anymore. As a result, ex-pinstripers are flocking to franchising."[5]

One can accurately gauge trends and the pulse of the American people by keeping an eye on advertisements. In the last few years the emphasis has been on getting back to basics, on the belief that the simple life is worth pursuing, and on the idea that relationships are more important than money. Now the ads are catering to the growing group of home workers. Even major computer companies are displaying advertising that picture a father by his computer interacting with his child, creating an atmosphere of warmth and compatibility between work and family pursuits.

And so they should. Currently, 26.6 million Americans work from home at least part-time, according to LINK Resources Corporation, a New York marketing research firm. That's 23 percent of the total labor force.[6] "The 1990's is the decade in which home-based business will finally be fully recognized as the economic force it really is," says Coralee Smith Kern, founder and director of the National Association for the Cottage Industry (NACI). "In Wyoming, Montana, and Idaho, 47% of all businesses are home-based. Home-based business is a multi-billion dollar market segment. That's a fact."[7]

With an uncertain economic climate, layoffs, recessions, and threats of depression, personal financial stability seems more uncertain than ever. In an effort to take more control over their financial future, many are laying the groundwork for starting a business or have already taken the plunge. "Ten years ago, working from home was considered a passing fad. Today, we believe it's the best hope for our economy."[8]

Market researcher George Barna echoes the trend. "The influx of new office technology at affordable prices has spawned a new work style: people working from their homes, either starting new businesses or working from the home at the request (and with the financial support) of their corporate employer."[9]

In less than a century, the drastic change of business power is seen in the fact that in "1900, 30% of the population was employed [whereas] 70% was self-employed. [In] 1980, 70% of the population was employed [whereas] 30% was self-employed."[10] We're not necessarily talking big business. "Fifty percent of the more than 11,000,000 firms in the U.S. have sales of less than $100,000 annually and employ fewer than 10 people!"[11]

Many levels of small business are laden with red-tape and bureaucracy. But for many persons it is worth overcoming the paperwork obstacles in order to gain the freedom that ownership offers. "Unquestionably, the growth of home offices has outpaced the capacity

of American Institutions—government and big business—to comprehend the importance of this phenomenon."[12]

KATHY'S STORY

Over twenty years ago I (Kathy) decided that one of my life goals was to be a published writer. However, due to family responsibilities (not to mention the inordinate amount of time packing, moving, readjusting, and making a new home for our family) and other obligations, I put this desire on hold. Although for many years I had read about and honed my craft, it was always in the back of my mind that when our youngest went off to first grade, I would devote my energies full-time to writing.

It was not to be. At the close of Dione's kindergarten year, Dave came home from his job an hour's commute away and announced that I needed to get a full-time job in the fall. The cost of living was more than we could handle if we wanted to keep the kids in a private school. I was crushed! For years I had held onto my dream, and now it was being dashed with no apparent hope of fulfillment. Not only that, but I loved being home. It was my domain, and the role of homemaker was fulfilling to me. Yet no amount of discussion could convince Dave that maybe we could make it without my going to work.

Jobs were scarce where we lived. Only the week before, hundreds were standing in line for the handful of positions at a new grocery store complex. Realizing I had no alternative but to get a job, I thought I had better start looking right away (spring) so that I would have something lined up for the fall. When I lamented my misfortune to a friend at that very same grocery store, she suggested that I ask to work at the bakery, as she had heard they were still hiring.

I figured it couldn't hurt. After a brief interview with the manager (during which time she found out I could do cake decorating), she stunned me by asking, "Can you start at eight tomorrow morning?" *Wait a minute! I don't even want a job—and especially not a day before I have to!* I told her I would call her later that afternoon and let her know. Dave, of course, encouraged me to accept the position immediately.

The next morning found me unprepared for the feeling of constraint I had at having to fit into the strange way of doing things at the bakery. We employees were treated as though we were mindless robots. Many at the bakery were all too eager to comply with unreasonable and unethical requests in order to gain favor with the manager. Others were inwardly pained in conscience but remembered their children at home, so said nothing. Over the next couple of days I found myself getting angry at the frequent injustices forced on helpless workers—workers who lived in fear of being once again without a job. (I didn't consider myself helpless—it didn't matter to me if I had a job.) The other workers didn't even want me to speak out on their behalf for fear of their getting fired.

It was Memorial Day weekend. We had had a family camping trip scheduled. However, due to my much-wanted new job, I had to stay home while Dave took the three girls on the trip. *Fun.* By now I had successfully completed three days on the job and was beginning the fourth. As I was lifting a stack of bread trays from a cart to transfer them to a counter, I misjudged their weight. (Big time!) As the trays crashed to the floor, I continued holding them, trying to break their fall. In doing so, I perforated a disc in my back. *Great. Now, not only do I have to work at a job I don't want, but I have to "hurt while I work."*

I went home that night with little use of my right side, thinking it would be better in the morning. Not so. The whole next day at the bakery I felt like crumbling in a heap of pain. With a grimace on my face and dragging my right side along, I tried to maneuver cake icing with uncooperative fingers. Later, at home, I decided to quit the job because of the pain. Dave happened to call and tell me what a good time they were having—while I was groaning in the background. When I told Dave I had to quit, he suggested that I see if workman's compensation would cover treatment. I had never heard of workman's comp, but the next day I learned I could put in a request. The doctor immediately pulled me off the job. As a result of a documented injury, I was able to receive workman's compensation for six months. It was enough to get us by—for then. Over the next several years, through muscle and physical therapy, I finally regained full use of my right side and only rarely have to deal with pain resulting from that injury.

As the six months of compensation pay drew to a close, the borough (similar to a county) mayor was running for the state senate. Since I had the same philosophical foundation as the mayor, after she won the primary I volunteered my talents in writing and designing promotional materials to help her get elected. Should she get elected and have to move closer to the government offices, she wanted me to manage her bookstore in her absence. Since the workman's compensation benefits were to end shortly, the offer came at a good time and sounded like an interesting job.

In the process of taking the mayor's promotional materials back and forth to the printer, I became acquainted with the printer, who was interested in my work. After asking me several times to talk to him about a position there, out of courtesy I lined up an interview. I was actually looking forward to managing the bookstore, so I had no interest in considering another job.

In discussing the options, Dave and I concluded that with my personality, the job with the printer would be more attractive. I would be on my own, set my own hours, and be able to advance quicker. So, after the campaign, I found myself selling printing and doing some writing and graphics. Since the mayor had won her election to the state senate, her mayoralty was now vacant. I decided the best way to get printing accounts was to approach each candidate in the upcoming special election. I would select one of the candidates and offer to write and design his or her promotional materials. Then

I would see if the other candidates were interested in having us print, but not write, their materials.

I had previously worked as a free-lance newscaster and had covered the borough assembly. As a result, I was familiar with several of the candidates. I made an appointment with the one I thought was the most qualified and asked to design and write the copy for his promotional materials. We met for one hour, after which he asked me to be his campaign manager. After the shock wore off, I told him I would think about it. I had three concerns. (1) Was this person someone I could back with integrity? (2) What about my job with the printer? I had only been working there a week. (3) I didn't know anything about managing political campaigns.

I decided that the candidate seemed to be someone I could endorse. Then I asked the printer if I could have the duration of the campaign off (six weeks). He said yes. Finally, I went to the library and checked out books on political campaigns. (Later the candidate I worked for said he thought I had had a lot of audacity in hesitating to represent him. After all, *he* was the one who was offering the position, and I should have been honored to have been asked.)

The candidate I represented was a political unknown who had been appointed to the borough assembly. He was running against a candidate who had just been defeated by the former mayor in the state senate race. The defeated candidate had statewide name recognition after having sunk more than $150,000 into the senate race, and was planning to put more into the mayor's race. The other major candidate had just lost a state house position, also had name recognition, and was quite well liked in the community. The two major candidates had been campaigning for months, and the mayor's race had become an extension of their earlier campaigns. We, on the other hand, had a budget of only about $4,000 and six weeks from start to finish to run a campaign (and try to win).

For six weeks I literally lived that campaign, sometimes working twenty hours a day. Dave did all the cooking, cleaning, laundry, and caring for the children in addition to working full-time with a two-hour daily commute.

The campaign was well-organized and was gaining tremendous momentum week by week. The night of the election I was confident that we had a fighting chance. It turned out to be one of the most devastating evenings I can remember. I took our candidate's loss personally. He lost by only 105 votes. For days afterward I kept thinking, *What could we have done to get those other few votes?* There was a run-off between the other two candidates I just mentioned (out of a field of six). We threw our support behind the underdog (the one who had run for the state house), and she won easily in the run-off.

As a result of that election, several other officials asked me to run their campaigns in upcoming elections. I had had enough of politics to last me many years, so I declined. Meanwhile, back at the printer, I hit the streets selling printing. During that time I was offered, either formally or informally, eight jobs in six weeks. And I didn't even want to be working! It was then that I began to get feedback about having skills that would be suitable for advertising and public relations. Several encouraged me to open my own marketing and public relations business. I wasn't even sure what one was, let alone know anything about the work. Then the printer started reinforcing the idea (he thought I could bring him more business if I had my own agency). Dave thought it was a good concept as well.

Hold it! Let's first check out some books from the library and see what an agency actually does. One weekend I read eight books on the subject and declared that I never wanted to own my own agency because it sounded like an incredible amount of pressure.

Continuing in that line of thinking, I was doing laps for physical therapy at a local high school pool. It was there that I met a lady who had just moved to our area. She had a degree in fine arts and had recently been offered a job with a New York ad agency, which she said was the epitome of ad agencies. Alas, she had to follow her husband's employment and gave up the opportunity in New York. Now here she was with all this skill . . .

About a week later I was in the print shop when a different young lady came in to make copies of her résumé. After small talk, we found that we hit it off and lined up a lunch date. As it turned out, she also had just moved to the area and had come with the intention of setting up her own ad agency. She had been in charge of the advertising and public relations of the largest theater in another state. At the moment, however, she was looking for a job until she could get to know the area better.

Lo and behold, the three of us formed a partnership. The first lady was to handle all the graphics, the second all the marketing and public relations projects, and I was to line up all the business, since I was familiar with the area (and because I didn't know the other aspects of the business).

Before we opened our doors, we had our first account, and that was enough to take care of all our start-up costs and bills for a month. We moved into a beautiful "A" frame office with large windows against a majestic backdrop. I had always wanted a "real" office. It turned out to be the best thing about the whole deal. All of the utilities were in my name since I had credibility in the area.

As far as naming the business, I wanted a generic, nondescript name. But my partners insisted that that wouldn't be very professional. So, after much discussion I agreed to use our last names. On the tail of that compromise, they hit me with another—the succession of names would sound the best with Babbitt first. *Wait a minute . . .*

After about a month of lining up clients so the other two could actually carry out the projects, we decided that they couldn't handle any more business. I would need to learn how to do what they did so that we could collectively produce more work. Monday morning I was to begin my training.

Up to this point all was running smoothly. But I started to notice some basic differences in business philosophy and ethics. These soon came to a head.

Monday morning the lady in charge of marketing and public relations chose to tell me that she was getting a divorce and she would be leaving the state in three days. Then the graphic artist dropped a bombshell. She had just discovered that she was expecting. Her doctor had told her that if she continued to work, she would lose the baby. She must pull back right away.

I was dumbfounded! I was angry! I was scared! We had signed contracts for the next year, and I didn't know anything about anything when it came to meeting those obligations. *How could they do this to me! What am I going to do now?*

In a blur of tears I went home and told Dave what had happened. The first thing he said was that I needed to give up the office (fortunately we were on a month-to-month basis). *Give up the office? It was the best thing about the business! I couldn't give up the office!*

OK, so wisdom won out. Dave built a beautiful desk in our second floor bedroom bay window overlooking a valley with a mountain peak in the distance. Beautiful. Then he installed a separate business telephone line and bought me an oak filing cabinet. The kids were getting out of school for the summer, so the timing coincided with my being able to be home with them.

The company name could easily shortened to Babbitt and Associates, as I had the intention of having other associates come on board in the future, in addition to Dave. (Two others actually did, but not as formal partners.)

I checked more books out of the library, asked a great many questions, and made some mistakes, but kept doing a project over and over until I got it right before taking it to the client. Each completed project gave me confidence and experience to tackle the next one. As a result of a potentially disastrous experience, my work won the most awards in the state for that year in marketing and public relations from a certain professional organization. It was only with God's help, encouragement from my husband, and terrific clients that it came to be.

CHOOSING A BUSINESS

There were positives and negatives at work in my situation. On the positive side, I had latent skills that worked well in marketing and public relations and we were in an area where our services could flourish. The market was ripe for allowing us to be successful. On the negative side, since my skills were undeveloped it perhaps would have been better to polish them before launching out to open a business. (Yet I had not intended nor expected to be forced into having to produce work I was unprepared for.) LESSON: Be prepared for the unexpected and improve the skills most necessary for success in your chosen field *before* you start your business. Be aware of the potential risks for liability (everything was in my name), and be sure to acquire proper licensing and zoning permits. LESSON: Avoid partnerships if at all possible.

What are your skills and abilities? Determine what you are good at as well as what you enjoy. Select a wide field, and then interview others already working in that field. At first it is best not to limit yourself to a specific specialty because in your research you may uncover an area you have not previously considered. Attend conferences, seminars, and trade shows relevant to your field of interest. What need will you be providing in your business? Do your market research. Find out what is already being done, how it is being done, how successful it is, and if there is room for you. Ask for help. Get the advice of a lawyer, accountant, or other business owners.

Here are some categories to consider: agriculture (lawn care, firewood, greenhouse), crafts, small maufacturing and repair, rubber stamps, clothing, shoe repair, upholstery, foods (baking, catering, school lunches, supper meals), merchandising and retail sales (mail order selling, books), paid services (desktop publishing, cleaning, sewing, teaching), and pet care. In addition, you could teach community classes in whatever skills you possess. Locally our community center pays $17.50 an hour for teaching classes, and you don't need a degree. Since this is the Midwest, I would assume that the remuneration would be higher in other areas of the country. The advantage to teaching is that you can set the days, hours, and duration of your class or classes. Teaching could provide you with seed money for your new business plus garner you contacts and credibility within the community.

Write a summary of what you want to accomplish through your business, a potential customer profile, and your target budget. Think creatively to offer a twist to an existing service or product. Instead of a typical office organization service, add workshops for the company's employees, a six-month check-up to iron out new frustrations, or a pick-up and delivery service for special projects you could do for the company from home (developing a master mailing list, sorting through years of back magazines for industry-related articles, or typing new labels for business files—projects regular office personnel have little time for but that could add to the efficiency of their business).

Or, instead of a run-of-the mill handyman service, develop a small booklet of the common types of jobs you deal with and explain how a person could do them himself. Then, when a larger need comes up, guess who they will call? Or you might write a column for your local weekly paper offering your expertise—again placing your name and business in front of the public as a competent person to contact when they have similar problems.

POSITIVE: I had the encouragement and emotional backing of others in the community as well as my husband to help over the rough spots. NEGATIVE: I gave up another job before testing the waters of the new venture. POSITIVE: First, we had adequate cash on hand to cover start-up costs and to get us through that first month with just one client. Therefore, we had absolutely no debt. Second, we had a relatively easy time building on that client base to bring in even more working capital. Third, Dave was bringing in the bulk of the family's finances, so the pressure on me was not that great. LESSON: If you plan to start a business, try to hang onto your current means of income while you get the business going on the side. Then you will be better able to determine if there is a market for your service or product. Your new venture must be able to support you minimally before you give up your other source of support.

By starting slowly, you can more readily avoid debt. "Very few businesses fail when they are out of debt. Most so-called business 'failures' are actually fledgling ventures shut down by impatient creditors."[13] When a business's liability is under $5,000 the percentage of failures is 4.6 percent, whereas a liability of $5,000 to $25,000 increases the rate of failure to 32.8 percent. The percentage increases even further, to 41.2, when the liability is from $25,000 to $100,000.[14]

Of all business failures, the percentage of failures of companies in business for five years or less is 53.2 percent. Businesses in operation six to ten years account for 24.4 percent. Those in existence over ten years make up 22.4 percent of the total failures.[15] "The experience and competence needed to make good decisions come only with time. . . . By starting and managing our own business without borrowing from strangers we [gave] ourselves the time needed to gain business experience and competence."[16] LESSON: Try to avoid debt when starting your business.

The Family Business Workshop holds seminars across the country and has resource materials available. We reviewed a taped presentation of the seminars and believe they are excellent from a Christian perspective. The address of the organization is P.O. Box 2250, Gresham, OR 97030; (503) 667-3942. Their emphasis is on beginning a family-owned business debt-free, or with the least amount of risk, and then applying key principles in developing that business.

Endeavor to retain your former employer as your client. He already knows your quality of work; he won't have to pay benefits, overhead, office space, and utilities; and he may only need your services part-time instead of paying a full-time salary. In times of recession you will find that being a consultant will be in your favor. "Seventy-seven percent report that their company has been adversely affect by the recession, with eighteen percent reporting 'very adversely affected.' . . . Sixty-two percent report that company staff has been lost or laid off during the recession. . . . Overall, the use of consultants has not changed during the recession for the majority of companies. Almost 49% report no change, while 27% report an increase in their use and 20% report a decrease."[17]

Continuously develop and refine your marketing strategy. Learn how to garner publicity for your business. Keep abreast of new developments in your field. Take or make the opportunity to learn all you can. Listen to your customers and respond to their needs. Become part of a network of like-minded business people and build up your support system. This will not only make your work more enjoyable, but you can gain additional business, be encouraged by others, and learn of new developments within the business community. Keep good records and maximize allowable tax deductions. Maintain a high level of integrity and practice healthy business ethics. Where possible, earn professional awards for your work to bring more credibility and recognition to your company.

Managing your own business will give you more self-confidence, foster pride in your accomplishments, and bring more enjoyment to the work you do. But be careful to preserve balance in your life and avoid the success mentality endorsed by many who have priorities that do not foster developing closer family relationships. In speaking of entrepreneurs, one author said,

> Their average work week is 75 to 80 hours. Entrepreneurs don't read many magazines. If junk mail gets to them, they fire the secretary. They watch less television than any other segment of the business world; they listen to almost no radio, except news and perhaps Rush Limbaugh. They are nonjoiners, nonvolunteers, and avoid anything that takes them away from their obsession with growing their companies. School plays and Little League games are a rare luxury. Cancelled vacations and broken dinner dates are part of their world.[18]

Throughout the article, the author hailed over 1 million entrepreneurs as unknown heroes. His perspective is completely opposite of the message we are trying to convey.

To help maintain a balance between your home-based business and family time, define your work hours and try to avoid making your business your life. Set realistic limits when you set up goals, and have a work plan for the day. There will always be one more project you can do to help your business thrive. However, at some point, the return diminishes on your time and effort. It is much better to use that "diminishing-return" time and energy with your family, where you can increase the investment in intangible rewards.

THE IMPACT OF
HOME-BASED BUSINESSES

Some states actively pursue legislation designed to help home-based businesses thrive. When a mass exodus of workers takes place in the states hardest hit by industry closures, valuable revenue leaves the state with them. States realize that the start-up phase of a business is as important as the period of continued growth. "Home businesses . . . are now seen as crucial to sustaining the social fabric of entire regions."[19]

Oklahoma's Lieutenant Governor, Jack Mildren, said, "If we want to keep people from leaving the state, we've got to develop a strong home-business network."[20] Oklahoma was the first state to organize an association to meet the needs of this group. Nick Sullivan, in an article on home businesses in *Home Office Computing,* says, "[The fact that associations like the ones in Oklahoma are] springing up across the country [is] yet another sign that home-based businesses, once a scattered grass-roots movement, are assuming a larger role in economic-development plans. . . . Home businesses are one of the keys to economic revitalization in the 1990's. What brought it home to me was seeing the interest of electric cooperatives in promoting home-business development."[21]

Marilyn and Tom Ross, in *Country Bound!*™, observe that in furthering this concept "some communities are actually launching sub-divisions targeted to *attracting* HBB's (Home-Based Businesses). Market Place in Oak Creek, Wisconsin, for instance, consists of 20 homes built especially to accommodate home occupations ranging from dentists' offices to craft studios. And each home in the Eagle-crest subdivision in Foresthill, California, was designed to include a teleport containing a personal computer and modem so occupants can link to computers—and employment!"[22]

RESOURCES

How to Run Your Own Home Business, by Coralee Smith Kern and Tammara Hoffman Wolfgram can be ordered from NTC Publishing Group, 4255 W. Touhy Ave., Lincolnwood, IL 60646–1975. The list price is $9.95 plus postage. Some of the topics the book covers are: "How to set up your business efficiently; how to run your business; how to market products and services; how to target new markets; how to best use banking, accounting, insurance, and other professional services; how to build and expand your business" (as stated on the back cover). This is only one of many books on the same subject. Your local library should have quite a selection as well.

The National Association for the Self-Employed provides benefits that are outlined in their promotional materials. These can be obtained by writing to the association at 2121 Precinct Line Road, Suite 100, Hurst, TX 76054 (telephone 1-800-232-6273).

Jeffrey Lant Associates produces a number of books that the small business owner may find helpful. Some of his resources overlap in the material, and they are more expensive than most. But they are thorough, well-researched, and full of practical help. The book we are currently reviewing is *How to Make a Whole Lot More Than $1,000,000: Writing, Commissioning, Publishing And Selling "How-To" Information* ($39.50 postpaid). This book is well worth the cost. You may want to check with your library to see if his materials are available. For a complimentary catalog of resources write to Jeffrey Lant Associates at 50 Follen Street, Suite 507, Cambridge, MA 02138.

As the trend of home-based businesses accelerates, more attention is being given to the undercurrent of dissension within the corporate world. In an article in the journal *Entrepreneur,* Janean Huber observes:

> Gigantic corporations are by nature unfeeling beasts. Employees are simply a means to an end, and humanity often comes in a distant second

place to the bottom line. In big business, that's just a fact of life. No wonder waves of ex-executives are defecting to entrepreneurship in general, and homebased business in particular. These veterans of the big business battlefield are a varied bunch. Some have been laid off or fired as a result of the recession; others are just plan sick and tired of the corporate game."[23]

How do these executives feel about the corporations they once belonged to? "Many former executives who make it past the adjustment stage would rather starve than hop back on the corporate ladder," Huber says. "Why the devotion to their homebased businesses? Because while America's conglomerates continue to provoke troubling questions, homebased businesses are providing a whole lot of answers."[24]

When we were in high school the oft-heard advice for young women was: "Go to college and get a degree in teaching. Then, if after you're married, your husband dies, you have something to fall back on to support yourself." The advice of the '90s for men or women would be: "Begin now to start and build up a home-based business so you have something to fall back on if you lose your job, change your priorities, or want to have more control over your personal economy." Millions of Americans are already on the way!

NOTES

1. "Seize the Future," *Success* 37, no. 2 (March 1990), 45.

2. "Career Moves," *Woman's Day*, 24 November 1992, 149.

3. Chart, *Home Office Computing*, August 1991, 43.

4. Marilyn Ross and Tom Ross, *Country Bound!™ Trade Your Business Suit Blues for Blue Jean Dreams* (Buena Vista, Colo.: Communication Creativity, 1992), 181. All quotes from this work are used by permission.

5. Carol Steinberg, "Corporate Dropouts Find Franchising," *USA Today*, 11 May 1992, 1E.

6. Mark Golin, Mark Bricklin, David Diamond, *Secrets of Executive Success* (Emmaus, Pa.: Rodale, 1991), 227.

7. Betty Fifer, "The Tidal Wave, The Home Based-Business Movement," News release from the Cottage Connection® (312-472-8116), 1–2.

8. Paul and Sarah Edwards, "The Home Office Comes of Age," *Home Office Computing* 10, no. 4 (April 1992), 26.

9. George Barna, *The Frog in the Kettle: What Christians Need to Know About Life in the Year 2000* (Ventura, Calif.: Regal, 1990), 99.

10. Gregg Harris, *The Home and Family Business Workshop* (Gresham, Oreg.: Christian Life Workshops, 1992), 2.

11. Ibid., 2.

12. Hugh Roome, in *Home Office Computing* 9, no. 12 (December 1991), 6.

13. Harris, 3.

14. Dun & Brandstreet, reported in Harris, 3.

15. Ibid., 4.

16. Harris, 4.

17. *National HRD Executive Survey, American Society for Training and Development,* February 1992, 1, 3.

18. "The Third Market: The Entrepreneurial Movement Will Save America," *Success* 39, no. 6 (July/August 1992), 9.

19. Nick Sullivan, "Rx for Rural Economies: Home Biz," *Home Office Computing* 10, no. 8 (August 1992), 96.

20. Ibid.

21. Ibid.

22. Ross and Ross, 260.

23. Janean Huber, "Free at Last," *Entrepreneur* 20, no. 9 (September 1992), 100.

24. Ibid., 105.

Things for Sale

PART 4

10

Things, Things, Things!

hat is an American? "A person who drives a bank-financed car on a bond-financed highway on credit card gas to open a charge account at a department store so he can fill his savings and loan financed home with installment purchased furniture," says one writer.[1] This brand of American is in dwindling supply today. He represents a bygone era of excesses and indulgence, tempered only by the lack of creativity in financing. It was the 1980s.

With this indulgent decade came the myth of prosperity. The mind-set was best summed up by *Newsweek:* "Our most profound illusion about prosperity was to think that great doses of it would solve almost any problem. We unwittingly adopted a view of human nature that assumed spiritual needs could ultimately be satisfied with material goods."[2] There is more to life than things. It is only recently that the American masses have been willing to acquiesce to this concept. They have spent their lives in a futile attempt to prove the myth's validity and ended up living in ghettos of affluence all across America.

A wealthy acquaintance is typical of those who have "arrived." He has all that money can buy—land, houses, cars, travel, entertainment, and expensive technological toys. But amidst a life of broken relationships he has an emptiness and fear of dying that all his power and worldly possessions cannot conquer. How about you? Are you trying to fill a void in your life through purchasing more and more things?

One doesn't have to be wealthy to be controlled by things. It is not uncommon for those who grew up in the depression to gather possessions around them in an effort to soothe the memory of past deprivations. Never again do they want to feel the ache for substance and necessities. Their "things" may not be the latest model or the fanciest style. But these people accumulate in abundance, nonetheless. Some of them accept too many of the cast-offs offered them. Others become scavengers at garage sales and auctions or fall victim to the pack rat syndrome. Persons with an obsession with accumulation find their security in living an illusion of plenty.

Materialism is not confined to Western societies. Even in Third World countries the quest for more is evident in the number of cows one has, or a bright square of cloth, or a piece of tin fashioned into an arrow. While we lived in Africa, we could see the scope of human emotions, desires, and frailties being played out on a stage far different from what we were used to—but the similarities in noncultural humanness could not be hidden or denied.

> No sooner had our crates arrived in Zaire than an African named Tatu was asking if he could buy our mini-bike when our three-year term was over. The mini-bike was barely visible in the two-by-four-foot packing crate. Shocked at the request, Dave answered, "We'll see." Little did he realize the breadth of Tatu's appeal.
>
> Some people think materialism is limited to the United States. But the longing for more indicates a heart condition. . . . It transcends one's culture and economic strata. In this case, Tatu became first enthralled with the idea of possessing a mini-bike; then enraptured by the desire to have it; next engulfed by the responsibility of owning it; and finally, enslaved to keeping it at all costs.
>
> At the end of our term, Dave faced a difficult decision. Knowing how Tatu would have to sacrifice, not only to buy the mini-bike, but also to keep it operating, Dave hesitated to sell it to him at all. But because Tatu had asked him before anyone else did, Dave felt obligated to honor the request.
>
> A few years later we learned that the overwhelming desire to own the mini-bike had become Tatu's undoing. Not content with a bicycle that was within his means, Tatu brought disgrace to his family, lost his job and his home provided as part of his salary, and ended up losing the mini-bike after all.
>
> Tatu had stolen from his employer to pay for the mini-bike and gas. But as time passed, Tatu couldn't even use it because parts weren't available. Tatu lost his dignity, respect from his family, and honor in the community—all for a thing.[3]

THE ACCUMULATION FACTOR

Shopping has become a national sport, with many participants and few spectators. Those who acquire the most possessions join the ranks of the prestigious in the winner's circle. Americans have made a pastime of consumption as entertainment. We have collected trivia that has become junk before it's even paid off. From this trinket to that toy, things tend to be an end in themselves instead of a means to a more fulfilling way of life.

The basis for an unceasing acquisition of things is often a spirit of discontent, pride, insecurity, greed, rejection, or emptiness. When was the last time you bought something you really didn't need but felt compelled to buy in order to fill a different kind of need through your purchase? In the end, did it satisfy?

Did you ever consider that there may be a correlation between the accumulation of things and our frantic lifestyle? We are so used to buying whatever we want, even if only on a small scale, that denying ourselves seems unthinkable. The busier we are, the less time we have to consider creative alternatives. It is easier to plunk down dollars or a credit card as we rush to the next activity than to evaluate the necessity of our purchase. If the hectic pace will not satisfy, then surely this new "thing" will. "People buy when they're discontent, envious, afraid, left-out, and obsessed with power or prestige. The materialism rampant in the baby-boom generation is not so much a sign of success but of desperation."[4]

The acquisition of things is addictive and progressive—addictive in that it becomes a habit even as one surrenders rational thought; progressive in that it takes more and more to satisfy, although the satisfaction is only superficial, masking the real need.

Are you driven to acquire more and more? Maybe you think you will never be caught in a web of desire for things. But temptation can strike when least expected. Kathy holds possessions loosely. That's why she was unprepared for the overpowering compulsion she once felt to purchase something that she wanted, and could even convince herself she "needed," but could absolutely not afford at that time.

It was during a period when Dave was unemployed. Our checking account was almost depleted. Bills were coming due and we had long ago used up any cash we had stashed away for small emergencies. The item in question was a $12 organizer/notebook combination. Every so often Kathy changes her notebook to replace a worn out or boring system, and she was past due for a change.

But the strength of that desire only increased because she knew there was no way she could possibly have it come to pass at that moment (credit aside). It bothered her that she could let a "thing" exert such a strong force on her desires. So she went home and prayed to be freed from the clutches of greed, or whatever emotion had taken over. Next she praised God for meeting our bills thus far. Then she gave her current system a face-lift to help thwart the desire for a new one.

It may be a more expensive item that has you feeling the same way. Evaluate why the desire is so strong, and try to find an alternative within your grasp. Change the subject in your mind when necessary, instead of dwelling on your immediate deprivation. Maybe even learn to be content to do without. Then if you are able to acquire the item in the future, you will appreciate it that much more. George MacDonald once said, "To have what we want is riches, but to be able to do without is power." Over the years, Kathy has noticed in her work helping women organize their homes and lives that women are able to let go of cumbersome habits in the same proportion as they are willing to let go of things.

Beyond the time consumed in earning money, shopping, and maintaining our excesses is the issue of investing emotional energy in things rather than people. It is often easier to spend time with inanimate objects than it is to relate to people through allowing ourselves to become vulnerable, or through being concerned with another's well-being rather than our own. The more we have, the more we tend to insulate ourselves from people.

Even children are encouraged to perpetuate accumulation. It comes with an abundance of Christmas gifts, extravagant birthday presents, continuous mall hopping, and a desire on the part of the parents to give their kids whatever they want. Kids are afraid of being different, and parents give things rather than instill in them the courage to be unique. This pressure to conform threads its way to adulthood and affects what we buy, what we do, and even how we think. Our culture is driven by the dollar and fed by mass insecurity through unscrupulous propaganda called advertising.

In *Kids Who Have Too Much,* Ralph E. Minear and William Proctor say that when parents give their children too much money they often are doing it out of guilt as a substitute for love and as an alternative to providing financial instruction. The result when children are given too much? It can be summed up in five "affluenza factors," Minear and Proctor say: (1) Children have lost a solid home foundation. (2) Adults see children as commodities. (3) Children are deteriorating physically. (4) Too many children are emotionally unhealthy. (5) Children have become too jaded.[5]

IS THERE LIFE AFTER THE MALL?

Yet, there is hope. The winds of change are spreading from one coast to the other. Americans are hungering for ways to cut back, buy less, use less, and waste less. "Things" have failed to come through on their glittering promises and fantasy marketing pitches.

One family's experience echoes the movement's variety.

> For six months we have lived in an 8' x 21' camp trailer on some property we bought. We had a well already on the property, but we have no electricity. (Our camper is all propane.) We have just purchased, with cash, a 10' x 55' mobile home early 60's model and that will be our home until we have our land paid for.

Every project, getting power, etc., is done totally through cash. I am a stay-at-home mom who home schools (two boys ages 9 and 12). We love it! Our property is 17 miles from the nearest town. Most people think we are crazy and strange to go without "many necessities" of life. The children and I have had fun watching birds, squirrels, chipmunks, deer, and porcupines.

Her husband says:

In the short run, it has been harder on us. But in the long run, the not too long run, like next spring, it will be easier. By paying cash for everything you are freer financially. It is hard to budget for big expenditures. But . . . buying things on time . . . puts you in financial bondage.

Although I have been foolish in the past concerning major purchases, I have learned to be patient—brutally patient, but it has paid off. For instance, when I needed a different vehicle, I saved for it and found a small truck for $500 that was a good deal because I had the cash on hand, and now I don't have to answer to a bank. There are lots of guys at work who have their big fancy toys, like snowmobiles, but it all weighs heavily on them.[6]

Think about *your* first apartment or rental home. Do you remember how much fun it was to fix it up with almost nothing? How satisfying it felt to create an atmosphere of warmth and homeyness out of this discard or that hand-me-down? From sanding and staining an old bookcase to trimming the windows with curtains made from worn sheets, the effect was something to behold. In one of our earlier apartments, we made an unusual array of furniture from sturdy orange crates discarded by a local fruit stand. These served us well through a number of moves during those long years when we were students.

Do you remember the progression of replacing those creative hand-hewn pieces and decorations for the up-and-coming store-bought counterparts? Sure, they were more trendy and chic. But we wonder if something wasn't lost in giving way to the demands of society to conform to a style, or in succumbing to the notion that newer is always better. With the new, did there not also come a chill across your living room? As the friendly pieces bid their farewell, did not the warmth of your early spontaneity and hospitality also bid farewell?

In all the homes we have visited over the years, the ones that bring a sense of fond remembrance are those that offered the warmest hospitality. Some were meager in material comforts, others quite lavish. It mattered not the size of the feast nor the state of the furnishings. What meant the most was the friendliness, care, and thoughtfulness to us as weary travelers or longtime friends.

Even the home furnishings industry is noticing the difference. In an article in the *Chicago Tribune,* Sharon Stagenes reports that "consumers apparently no longer yearn for the fast-track lifestyle with flashy, high-fashion furnishings that typified the 1980's. They are opting instead for comfortable, casual classics and homes resembling a casual weekend retreat."[7]

We once moved from a four-bedroom house into a two-bedroom apartment. This forced us to take stock of the things that were the most important to us, as opposed to the things that just took up space. It felt good to finally let go of those "somethings we might need someday." If we didn't have room, it went. Life became so much simpler by our not having to walk around, clean, store, or sort an excess of "things."

Does your environment bring a sense of peace and order, or does it overwhelm you with confusion, disorder, or maybe even unnecessary extravagance? Is your equilibrium disturbed or balanced because of what you own? What about your personal stress level? Are your possessions creating a vague inner tension? Have you become dependent on material proof of your worth? Charles Spurgeon once said, "It is not how much we have, but how much we enjoy that makes happiness." The less we need in order to be happy, the less control things have over us.

We have some friends from Alaska who have nine children. Every few years they take a two-month trip to "the outside," or "lower 48." Each child has a small duffel bag, smaller than the size of an average gym bag. The family has a fine-tuned system to keep its travels and visits enjoyable. It never ceases to amaze us how little this family of eleven can get by with for two months on the road. They have a car top on their van, but no trailer. They make relationships among themselves and with their friends a top priority and become an encouragement to others wherever they go.

Before you make a purchase, even a small one, consider the implications. Will it draw your family together, or will it cause undue pressure by creating disunity either in terms of cost or use? What are your motivations—to impress others, lift a sagging ego, dispel boredom, meet a real need, enhance a life goal, or bring another joy? Are you enjoying what you already own or have you tired quickly with your last purchase?

As a mental exercise, if you were in a situation where you could only keep three things besides your car, home, and photo albums, what would they be and why? When Kathy drew this question years ago as a part of a game her answers were: sewing machine, typewriter, and kitchen center. To her, they were an extension of her creativity as well as tools to further goals she had for her life at that time. What about you? When you are tempted to make a purchase just for something to do, instead embrace a sunset, linger with a magazine, extend a helping hand to your elderly neighbor, or make your kid's favorite dessert from scratch. And then think about it: Which had the greater capacity for bringing satisfaction?

Maxine Hancock, in *Living on Less and Liking It More,* says:

> The call to reconsideration of our life-style is being pressed upon us by a number of economic facts: recessions, inflation, the clamorous needs of the third world. It is a call which is being issued by politicians as well as preachers. The Canadian Prime Minister recently called on the Canadian people, "not for sacrifice, but for restraint." . . . We sit in our living rooms and look into the "unseeing eye" of our television sets and see not just individuals but entire cities and nations going bankrupt. And at the same time we look into the empty eyes of swollen-bellied children of famine who are somehow, impossibly, still alive. And we know that somewhere, in some way, we are all personally responsible. . . . Any cinching in of our belts that we undertake will not, in the long run, hurt any of us. It is very often only when we begin to feel pinched economically that we start to sort out the debris of our things-cluttered lives and decide which things are really important and which are peripheral.[8]

DETHRONE YOUR STUFF
AND DECLUTTER YOUR SPACE

When our homes are rampant with runaway clutter, it is hard to enjoy a sense of peace and order. With all of the books available on home organization, we have the resources to keep that same stuff organized. But how much freer life would be if we didn't *have* so many things to organize. Seeing so much stuff day after day erodes simplicity in thought and living. Consciously or subconsciously, when we are surrounded by an overabundance we tend to feel more out of control and our minds are bombarded by unnecessary preoccupations.

The first step in simplifying our world of things is to dethrone our "stuff" and its importance in our lives. A subtle root of discontent can plague even the most astute. Absorbing advertising regularly, forming comparisons with others, greed, lack of meaning, pride, and the feeling that "something better has got to be out there" all lead to a spirit of discontent. How quickly an acquired "thing" loses its ability to satisfy. The greater the expectation before acquisition, the greater the letdown afterward. When was the last time you had a feeling of deep satisfaction? Was it when you bought something, or was it when you gave of yourself to help another? Which required the greater sacrifice? Was it worth it? What do your possessions mean to you? Are you placing them on the throne of your little world? Do you have a compulsion in any area (clothes, hobbies, electronic equipment, furnishings) to acquire things? Have those "things" taken the place of relationships in your life?

As long as we allow things to control our desires and dreams, we will not be able to free ourselves from the clutches of discontent. Often we use things as a substitute for faltering relationships and lack of purpose in our lives. In *Surviving Life in the Fast Lane,* Tim Kimmel says:

> Keeping the average family discontent is vital to our economic system. In order to lure me to a particular product, an advertiser must create a dissatisfaction for what I have—or a nagging desire for what I don't need. In order to be content we must learn to discipline or control our desires. When people fail to discipline their desires, they feel incomplete. A gloomy cloud of inadequacy follows them around. It's difficult to maintain deep relationships with such people—their feelings of inadequacy drain your emotions. When people fail to control their desires, they give into the powers in the world system that desire to control them.[9]

The last chapters of this book will show you how to banish discontent on its deepest level. But for now, take hold of the idea that you are going to abandon your craving for acquisition and dependence on things as a way of finding happiness.

Once you have committed to dethrone the position of "stuff" in your life, you will be free to declutter your space. Anything that detracts or distracts from who you are or what you want to be can be considered clutter. If newspapers strewn about makes you feel intellectual and gives a homey remembrance of days gone by when your father spent time reading you the daily paper, then maybe for you those newspapers are not clutter. But to the person whose equilibrium is disturbed by those same newspapers, those newspapers are clutter.

Begin by asking yourself, "What is clutter for me?" List the areas of your home or office that cause irritation. Keep in mind that often we can live with clutter because that is all we have ever known. Until we live in an orderly home, or function with a clean desk, we will not know what we have been missing. Sometimes the desire to abandon clutter comes from a heightened sense of self-respect to know that we can have the discipline to keep an orderly home or office. Or it may come from wanting to eliminate the frustration of looking for something and not being able to find it without a lengthy search. It may be motivated by a desire for increased enjoyment in having our children bring their friends over to visit. Have your children been making excuses for not doing so? Could it be because they are embarrassed at the state of affairs, either physical or emotional, in your home? Or the motivation to declutter may be borne out of love for a mate who seems so much happier when the home is clutter-free.

In some individuals, clutter actually meets needs. It may be a smoke screen covering a fear of entertaining, the rationale being, "If my home is a mess, then I don't have to invite people over." Until clutter is actually removed, we may not be aware that it has had such a grip on our lives. Perhaps you are holding onto living in a disorganized mess because you fear that if you did clean it up, you couldn't keep it that way. Maybe the fear of not being able to continually meet expectations keeps you chained to a way of life you find neither enjoyable nor profitable.

Clutter produces stress both at low and high levels: at low levels by daily puncturing our sense of peace in our surroundings, creating an inner tension we may not even be aware of; and at high levels through the turmoil created when we cannot find something very important we need *right now*. Family conflicts seem to rear their ugly heads more often when our homes are in a state of disorder than when they are pleasant and neat. Clutter gives a feeling of being out of control that can wreck havoc with our steady progression through life.

Realize that certain times of the month or year you will be more able to motivate yourself to get rid of things that you don't really need: after the Christmas season, when you have already garnered momentum by putting away decorations and cleaning up pine needles; during the newness of spring when you've swung open the windows and the scent of change is in the air; in the fall with the new school year and the settledness that accompanies routine. What you weren't willing to dispose of last year can today be loosened easily from your grip. On the first pass through your house in an effort to decrease the amount of things you clean, sort, put away, step over, or get angry with, try decreasing your inventory by 10 percent. Even that will make a substantial difference in how bogged down we feel with an excess of things.

We received a letter from an elderly lady who heard us on a radio broadcast.

> My problem is this: After 70 years of being a "Pack Rat" you can imagine my apartment, car, pocketbook and even my mind are *overrun* with good and bad. I never had enough of anything as a kid, and as I grew older, I started *gathering things*. If one was all I needed two must be better and now two in all colors and sizes, etc., etc., etc. . . .
>
> I now have practically all I need of most everything, but I can't even find it; so I have to go out and buy another, which very shortly gets lost in the jungle. What a vicious circle, and here I sit in the middle of it all; totally *overwhelmed!* I remember my grandmother's words, "A place for everything and everything in its place." Such wisdom. Now I have no places, they are all packed with accumulations. Yet the pattern has been set; when feeling frustrated and hopeless, I escape it and get out for a while. You guessed it, I find such a bargain some place. I buy it and bring it home.

Reading her letter makes Kathy want to get on a plane and help her wade through the years of accumulation and eliminate things —and then organize and arrange attractively what's left.

Be forewarned that when you go through the surgery of dethroning your stuff or decluttering your space other emotions may come into play that you didn't expect. Barbara DeGrote-Sorenson and David Allen Sorenson say in *'Tis a Gift to Be Simple:* "There is a great feeling of freedom in cutting back our consumption, but often grieving is part of the process, too. Embarrassment and low self-esteem may surface when we begin to rebuild our sense of self not from our possessions or our power to buy them but from a new set of values that asks only for our 'fair share.'"[10] But in the end, you will be happier for having done so.

NOTES

1. Howard Dayton, Jr., *Your Money: Frustration or Freedom* (Wheaton, Ill.: Tyndale, 1979), 39.

2. Robert J. Samuelson, "How Our American Dream Unraveled," *Newsweek*, 2 March 1992, 38.

3. Kathy J. Babbitt, *Habits of the Heart: Self-Discipline for the Not-So-Disciplined* (Brentwood, Tenn.: Wolgemuth & Hyatt, 1990), 109–10.

4. Bob Welch, *More to Life Than Having It All: Living a Life You Won't Regret* (Eugene, Oreg.: Harvest, 1992), 16.

5. Ralph E. Minear and William Proctor, *Kids Who Have Too Much* (Nashville: Thomas Nelson, 1989), 107, 28, 31, 32, 35, 38.

6. "Letter of the Month" (originated from Washington State), *Downscaling 46510*, December 1992, 7.

7. Sharon Stangenes, "A Rose Is a Rose," *Chicago Tribune*, 9 February 1992, sec. 15, 3.

8. Maxine Hancock, *Living on Less and Liking It More* (Chicago: Moody, 1976), 140, 145, 146.

9. Tim Kimmel, *Surviving Life in the Fast Lane* (Colorado Springs: NavPress, 1990), 62.

10. Reprinted by permission from *'Tis a Gift to Be Simple* by Barbara DeGrote-Sorenson and David Allen Sorenson, copyright © 1992 Augsburg Fortress, 24.

11

When Is Just Enough, Enough?

Dream with me a moment and visualize what you your life would be like if you could have all you wanted, be all you wanted, and do all you wanted. Now think through expansions that might take place in your life today. Say you just received a promotion. Do you envision yourself one day holding an even more prominent position? Or perhaps you just bought a new house. Do you see it filled with the latest furnishings? Maybe you recently graduated from college with honors. Is there a doctorate down the road for you? Or perhaps you won the 5K in the master's division last year. Will you aim for a 10K this year?

Kathy tried this exercise after her first book was published. All of a sudden success took on new proportions. In order to make her mark she thought about how many books she would have to publish to really stand out. When she found that some authors have published over a hundred books in a lifetime, the numbers factor was obliterated. Then she thought through what it would take to publish one book a year, plus speaking engagements for fame and fortune. All that came to mind was the tremendous amount of work that would be involved.

So she set her sights a little lower and thought about maybe just writing *one* other book—and quickly realized she didn't really care if she went through the process again. For twenty years her long-term goal was to someday have a book published. In spite of many necessary diversions along the way, she read, wrote, and took classes to hone her skills. But now that her dream had finally come about, she realized that it didn't actually matter to her if she reached another rung of the publishing ladder. She was content. It had been important to her to go through the process of completing the project and put organization to the thoughts that had been swimming in her brain for many years. But now that those thoughts had been expressed, she no longer needed to daydream about the ultimate extension of this part of her life. For her, enough was enough. She would enjoy her sense of contentment in the present and not put it on hold until a future venture came to pass.

If you are an advertising representative, do you dream about landing the biggest account ever? As a teacher, do you long for the day when you will be the head of your department? Or as a factory worker do you have your sights on becoming a supervisor one day?

Although goals are effective and excellent motivators, the fallacy is in thinking we cannot be happy until we have "arrived" at some future point of accomplishment. Just as Kathy realized how fruitless it was to postpone contentment until she made a mark in the record books for authors, so too is it foolish to deny ourselves the beauty of appreciating the present. If each of the scenarios in your mind actually came about, would you really be happier than you are right now? Why or why not? There may be things about your situation you could change immediately that would make life more enjoyable for you—stopping your participation in an unethical practice, showing more consideration for people, overcoming your tendency to procrastinate. But for the most part, all of us can reach the point where we are content in who we are and the work we do *right now.* Our ceaseless striving for advancement and recognition to the detriment of family relationships causes us to cry out, "Enough is enough!"

Balance comes to our lives through making conscious decisions: deciding to play a game with your son rather than to watch another hour of television; deciding not to buy that new car in order to pay off your credit cards; deciding to decline yet another leadership role and investing that time with your family instead; deciding to forego that extra degree and spend two years overseas aiding in humanitarian relief projects.

Good decisions come as a result of well-thought-out priorities. As you think about the areas of your life that need to be brought into

proper perspective, consider what need you are trying to meet through overindulgence in that area. Maybe it is a need for security, comfort, self-esteem, significance, or friendship. Think about creative alternatives.

WHAT IS JUST ENOUGH FOR YOU?

In spite of all the lamenting about the tough economical climate, "the average American still has more, does more, eats more, and experiences more than most of the people in the world. Along with the more mentality we have also come to expect more and want more."[1]

Some changes in this pattern are taking place, but it is slow going. In *Going Nowhere Fast,* Melvyn Kinder says that "the members of the baby boom generation . . . are not going out as much and are trying to scale down, but nonetheless, they are having great difficulty letting go of needs that have become part of their life. They also find themselves struggling with their rarely questioned value systems. These are hopeful signs, but the tyranny of money has long teeth and won't be shaken easily."[2]

Bob Welch, in *More to Life Than Having It All,* says, "Materialism consumes anyone who becomes obsessed with the value of purchased goods at the expense of relationships or giving to others.

In a time when 40,000 children a day die of malnutrition and disease in Third World countries, 52% of Americans—people with the highest collective standard of living in the world—say they daydream about being rich."[3]

Money

Decades of propaganda have convinced us that our self-worth is tied up in how much money we can make and spend. Kinder notes that

> money has wormed its way into the center of our psyches. Over the years the value of everything in our lives has come to be measured by a single monetary standard. If we want to know the value of a car, a service, or a work of art, we ask the same question: How much did it cost? Finally we have come to value our own self-worth by the same standard, by our capacity to make and spend. . . . Until we take back the power we have invested in money and divest it of its myriad meanings, we will unceasingly pursue it, for we will never have enough. Money is a fickle god—it seems to bring you closer to the rewards it promises, but never close enough for satisfaction, because the joy is fleeting, soon replaced by emptiness and the need for more.[4]

The quest for more money has eroded relationships, consumed emotions, wasted lives, twisted reality, demanded compromises, belittled integrity, and ruined health. Yet the dream that money will make us happy propels many to the brink of destruction—discovering, often too late, that it was all a facade. Oh, if they could live their lives over, many a rich person would tell you of the fruitless striving for this thing called wealth—how it never really satisfies, how it has caused them to sacrifice joys and sources of real happiness, how it was maddeningly empty and futile and in the end proved them to be a greater fool than they ever thought possible.

But many of us are like a rebellious teenager. "You lived your life and made your mistakes. It won't be like that for me. And if it is, let me find out for myself!" It is only through experiencing defeat and discouragement ourselves that many of us listen to the wisdom of the ages, but often we listen too late. What about you? Whose value system are you following? Does money make you feel more important? If you had nothing, would you feel just as secure in who you are as a person? "Just when you think you have enough, hardships can take it away or you can unexpectedly lose it in a financial crash. Security is an elusive goal."[5] (In later chapters we will discuss how you can find security aside from affluence.)

Savings and Investments

In order to help with expenses, pay off debts, and put more into savings, 7.2 million people work multiple jobs. With the trendy emphasis on increasing savings and investment portfolios, we can sometimes get carried away in planning for the future and ignoring the needs of others today. If stashing away funds to the exclusion of all else creates blindness with regard to the rest of the world, then maybe those dollars are causing personal depletion rather than growth. When was the last time you gave some of your money to church on a regular basis? Or helped the family down the street whose bread-winner became unemployed? Or were moved to compassion for the hungry around the world? Or tried to relieve the ongoing burden of a single mother?

Determine what you need each month to provide adequately for the future, and then let loose of some of your riches to make the world a better place for someone else today. Or, better still, designate a set amount each month to be given away *before* you think of yourself. That helps us appreciate much more what we do have and reminds us that all we own belongs to God.

The pursuit of money leads us away from our true goals. Kinder says:

> Having money can make you feel more secure than not having money, but ultimately security is an inner state of mind. Money can always be lost. When we create, in our mind, an equivalency between having money and having love, security, and power, then the pursuit of money becomes an illusion. The pursuit becomes a treadmill because we never get what we really want; with these misdirected efforts for well-being, all we get are deceptive imitations.[6]

Insurance

With the ever-present threat of lawsuits; personal tragedies of fire, death, floods, or tornados; medical contingencies; automobile accidents; business blunders; or unemployment, it's no wonder Americans are insurance-crazy. With the competent counsel of someone you trust, determine your realistic insurance needs. Is too large a portion of your budget going to this area? We can never really be fully prepared for what might happen in our lives. By going overboard in premium payments unnecessarily, we tie up funds that could be used more beneficially elsewhere. Again, balance is the key. Be sure to talk it over with a professional, maybe even several, whom you respect.

House

Now that you finally got your raise you can start looking around for a more upscale dwelling. The new subdivision seems to be just the place. With its lavishly landscaped yards, elegant homes, and modern amenities, it will surely make your family happy. Yes, the payments will eat up more than your raise, but you figure you could work overtime to make up the difference . . .

Hold it! First think through why you want to move. Is your house too small? Would remodeling do? Is it important for you to be considered "somebody"? There are other, less costly ways of bolstering a sagging ego. Are you convinced that you will be happy with a newer home? Real happiness is not dependent on surroundings. If you are not happy in your home now, chances are happiness will elude you in a newer one as well. Just ask some of the wealthy what role money has played in giving them a sense of true happiness.

Perhaps you want a healthier location for your family. Is your neighborhood dangerous or too crowded and you long for a place in the country? You don't have to spend all your waking hours paying for a showplace. By wise planning, you could get your country setting and have lower payments than you do now. It might take some labor on your part to fix a place up, but in the end you would come out ahead. Or are you simply tired of the same old walls? Then give them a face-lift with wallpaper, or change the furniture around. Is it not enough to spruce up what you have, rather than jeopardizing future funds for a place that may be just as boring a few years from now? How large a house will you have to buy before it is just enough for you?

Americans are starting to get the picture—that happiness is not owning a larger home. "The median size for a new home fell to 1,890 square feet last year, down from 1,905 in 1990, the first decline in 10 years." Amenities such as central air conditioning, two and a half baths or more, one or more fireplaces, a two-car garage or more, and a lot size of 22,000 square feet or more all decreased with new homes for the first time in years.[7] Not only are we lowering our housing expectations, we are making strides toward total debt reduction. "Last year, for the first time since 1958, consumers paid off more debt than they took on."[8] Even stores that feature bridal registries are reporting a no-nonsense approach to life. Brides-to-be are requesting the more mundane and sensible items in lieu of china and silver. They have seen that fancy things didn't help their parents' marriage and are opting to try a different path. Some of this cutting down on excesses was due to the recession, but a recession has a way of pruning our wants from our needs.

Furnishings

What goes into a house may not seem as big an expenditure as a mortgage, but some people easily make it that: new carpeting installed before the old is worn, a living room set replaced because a trendier color and style came out, appliances updated to the models with the latest computer settings, and custom-made drapes taking the place of last year's custom-made blinds. As you look around your home, is there never a time when you don't want more? Do you imagine this room with a new hutch or that room with an oriental rug? At what point will you be content with what you have? Sure, a new piece of furniture can do wonders for a room, or just the right decoration can give it that special touch. But to never be satisfied *until* you have your home just the way you want it will leave you in dissatisfaction limbo.

Education

Does the road ahead seem to be all school the rest of your life? What is your motivation for getting yet another degree? Will it really help in your profession, or is it an ego thing? Are you going to school to get away from a bad marriage? School can offer a false sense of security and be an escape from handling the really deep issues. Is the return on that costly private college really worth the tens of thousands of dollars it will cost you (or your parents)? When will you be able to say, "It's enough—let's get on with living"?

Education is important, no question about it. But again, when for most of your life school seems to be the only thing worth living for, then something is out of kilter. Reevaluate why you seem to be addicted to taking "just one more course." You may uncover some motivations that should be addressed in another way.

Friends

How many close friends do you have? Ones that you feel comfortable with in silence or conversation. Or are most of your friends acquaintances you have to wear a mask in front of? Sometimes we have the mistaken notion that having many friends is a visible testament to our worth. Flitting from one friendship to another may make us feel popular and may help to bolster us when we are down, but how many of those kinds of friendships do you need to be happy? Think about your most rewarding relationships. Are they superficial or genuine? Are you afraid of allowing someone to know the real you on the grounds that they might not accept you? When will you stop searching for that "ideal" friend and appreciate the ones you have? More is not better.

Clothes

"You are what you wear." How many times have we heard this adage? But are we really? No wonder the clothing industry does so well. It feeds on an erroneous value system. If who we are is tied up in what we wear, few of us would find relief from a low self-image. Taken to the extreme, we could easily be consumed by buying, changing, and wearing clothes. If clothes were all we had to measure our worth, there would be a steady stream of apparel from the stores to our closets. Some Americans are living like this now. Are you? How full does your closet have to be for you to feel good about yourself?

At one time, Kathy enrolled in a three-month language course in Europe. It seemed the university professor wore the same shirt and sweater for several weeks at a time. (Probably washed on weekends.) In our culture it is foreign to our thinking to wear clothes even for a few days in a row. But where we lived in Europe, clothes were expensive, there was a lack of washing machines, and the weather did not always cooperate for drying.

Think of how much time you could save in a week if you didn't have to shop for and accessorize a variety of outfits and then try to decide which to wear each morning. Even if we cut our repertoire of clothing in half, most of us would still have an abundant selection. The good news is that people are changing the habits they developed in the age of excess—even kids are getting back to basics and buying less expensive tennis shoes. The once highly acclaimed name brands have lost some of their appeal against the backdrop of shifting values toward the real and away from the superficial.

Entertainment

George Barna observes in *The Frog in the Kettle* that "many adults devote greater concentration and effort to making the most of their leisure hours than they commit to their productivity on the job. . . . We are driven by our leisure appetites. It is increasingly common to hear of people turning down job offers because the hours or other responsibilities would interfere with their hobbies, fitness regimes, and other free time activities. Even our spending habits show that playing has become a major priority. The average household spends more on entertainment than it does on clothing, health care, furniture, or gasoline."[9]

What is the purpose of entertainment for you? To escape, indulge, or enjoy? Or to build closer relationships? Is your leisure time consumed with selfishness or kindness? Are your amusements putting you further into debt? Can you think of creative alternatives that will not cause disunity in your family and still bring you enjoyment?

Sports

Whether as spectators or participants, some of us get carried away with this one. How much of your life is dedicated to watching, playing, talking about, thinking about, or coaching sports? Do you have an unhealthy emphasis on sports that disregards the people most important to you? Could you cut back your involvement and be just as content? On the other hand, even if you increased the amount of time spent on sports, would it make you any happier? Where do you draw the line? Have you ever thought about and made a rational decision as to the extent of your preoccupation? What would be just enough for you?

Cars

What goes on inside your head (or heart) when you see the latest model of sports car you have always admired? Does it cross your mind to acquire one someday, whatever it takes? What emotional charge do you get from having the biggest, fastest, shiniest car on the block? Is that catered-to feeling of a rich interior worth seeing your family get further behind on doctors' or dentists' bills? Does the roar of a big motor puff you up? If you dare, consider what motivations were behind your last car purchase or the one you are planning. Which features are at the top of your concerns: looks, economy, power, room, dependability, usefulness, or resale value?

Would those things most important to you be just as easily met through a used car rather than a new one? How far gone is your current vehicle? Is it still meeting your needs? How close is it to the scrap heap? A greater number of the American people are opting to keep their cars a few more years as they revise the "throw away" mentality prevalent in the '80s. Even the auto makers are streamlining their selections. In an effort to reduce manufacturing costs and to market to the growing "back to basics" segment, options are shrinking for the potential car buyer. What does your car say about you?

Consider selling your second or third car. We sold one of our cars shortly after we moved to this location. In addition to the sum of cash we received after the payoff was made, our actual savings were $211 per month in payments with two years left, $225 per year in tags, and $800 per year for insurance with good driving records and multicar discounts in a rural area. We also save on gas and maintenance costs by using only one vehicle.

Recognition

The quest for fame is played out in workplaces all across the country. From competing for awards to vying for management positions, the search for recognition is alive and well. The only problem is, those whose self-images are the most intertwined with public acclaim are the ones whose lives are the most fragile should it all crash around them.

Fathers who spend inordinate amounts of time at the office trying to impress a superior and hoping for a promotion are exchanging a potential reward for a sure thing at home. If these same fathers would put as much effort into developing family closeness as they do their work, they would find the affirmation they so desperately long for.

And if mothers would be as insistent on creating warmth in their homes as they are on achieving equality at work, families would not be in as much trouble as they are today. How much honor before the world do you need in order to be content with who you are as a person?

Food

"Undertakers report that human bodies do not deteriorate as quickly as they used to. They believe that the modern diet contains so many preservatives that these chemicals tend to prevent rapid decomposition after death."[10] That is the assessment of the *Farmer's Almanac.* We are presented on all sides with healthy alternatives to the rich, high-fat, high-calorie foods we grew up on. From whole grains and natural foods to low-fat selections, maintaining a healthy diet is more plausible today than in the past. This trend is making it somewhat easier for those who really *want* to control their eating.

Then there are those who think they want to control it, but don't. The vast amount of reading material on this subject makes it hard to offer the excuse that one lacks know-how. What is lacking is the will and the self-discipline to carry through. Isn't it about time you said, "Enough is enough," and just *did* it?

Shopping

How many days a week do you go near the stores? If you work, perhaps you are bombarded daily with designer windows beckoning you inside. Or maybe you work in a mall and are surrounded by the pull of materialism. Like two magnets in close proximity, you and shopping can be separated only if you make the extra effort to resist the pull.

You willingly submit to the advertiser's lure, thinking, *I'll just look today,* and then succumb to using your faithful credit card, all the while telling yourself, *Next time I'll do better.* In *When Spending Takes the Place of Feeling,* Karen O'Connor has this to say:

Most shopping addicts are living out someone else's "should system"—their mother's, a celebrity's, a manufacturer's, a designer's, a friend's. They are dealing with psychological and social influences so great they cannot even consider them, much less face and deal with them. Issues of low self-esteem, lack of boundaries, and problems with reality are all part of the complex behavior that plays itself out in a shopping frenzy.[11]

When we use shopping as a panacea for solving our problems, to mask feelings of hurt or rejection, or to fill an insatiable emptiness, the result will only be more grief, guilt, and loss of control. (If you sense you are addicted to shopping, the book just mentioned, *When Spending Takes the Place of Feeling,* may be of help to you. It is an excellent work that discusses many forms of overspending and the subsequent recovery process. Until underlying issues are taken care of, just saying no may not be enough to conquer this particular excess.)

On the positive side, there has been an alteration in buying habits over the last few years. Erika Kotite, in an article in *Entrepreneur,* says,

Shoppers aren't responding as well to the old trick of big, splashy markdowns; they know they can find the same merchandise elsewhere for even less. They insist on both quality and low prices. They know competition between stores is fierce, and they're taking full advantage of it.[12]

Despite some talk of an economic recovery, the recession continues to bring hardship to many consumers. Their confidence repeatedly battered by steady layoffs, news of failing banks, a mounting national debt and a weakening dollar abroad, Americans are shopping more frugally.[13]

We often think we are doing our kids a favor by giving them an abundance of money, things, freedom and independence, and responsibilities. But when we do that we are often handing them demise in disguise. An excellent book on this issue is *Kids Who Have Too Much,* by Ralph E. Minear and William Proctor (Thomas Nelson, 1989).

Barbara DeGrotte-Sorenson and Allen Sorenson have this to say about downscaling in their book *'Tis a Gift to Be Simple:*

Voluntary simplicity does not mean we all have to sell our homes. It doesn't even mean we can't have nice things. It may mean that we can't have all of them. Like anything else, however, it does require a beginning. Moving down is like putting a pencil to our life's story and asking, "What can I cross out and still have an abundant life? What excess can I remove from my life that will help me express my true values? What parts of my life's story are distractions that only keep me off pace and running ragged?"[14]

It takes wisdom and courage to be able to say, "Enough is enough." As Americans collectively and individually make the choice to have moderation in consumption, they will find a freedom from excess that ultimately leads to a more satisfying life.

NOTES

1. Kathy Babbitt, "When Is Just Enough . . . Enough?" *Downscaling 46510,* November 1992, 1.

2. Melvyn Kinder, *Going Nowhere Fast: Step Off Life's Treadmills and Find Peace of Mind* (New York: Fawcett Columbine, 1990), 80.

3. Bob Welch, *More to Life Than Having It All: Living a Life You Won't Regret* (Eugene, Oreg. Harvest House, 1991), 189.

4. Kinder, 80–81.

5. Ibid., 83.

6. Ibid., 84.

7. Bill Montague, "Builders Shrink House Plans," *USA Today,* 8 May 1992, 4B.

8. Mark Memmott, "The Economy: Paying for the Part," *USA Today,* 12 February 1992, 5B.

9. George Barna, *The Frog in the Kettle: What Christians Need to Know About Life in the Year 2000* (Ventura, Calif.: Regal, 1990), 82.

10. *Farmers' Almanac, 1993,* ed. Ray Geiger, Philom. (Almanac, 1992), 1.

11. Karen O'Connor, *When Spending Takes the Place of Feeling* (Nashville: Thomas Nelson, 1992), 73.

12. Erika Kotite, "Rethinking Retail," *Entrepreneur* 20, no. 12 (December 1992), 97.

13. Ibid., 98.

14. Reprinted by permission from *'Tis a Gift to Be Simple* by Barbara DeGrotte-Sorenson and David Allen Sorenson, copyright © 1992 by Augsburg Fortress, 16.

12

Spending Satisfies —Or Does It?

The annual spawning of Alaskan salmon is a sight to behold. In the rivers and streams, bays and inlets, they are so plentiful it is possible to wade into the waters and catch them bare-handed. One year Dave flew salmon from the beach (landing and taking off from the shore) at Bristol Bay to the processing plant some distance away. Making it a true family experience, we pitched our five-man base-camp tent on the treeless tundra. Kathy was the cook for a group of fishermen while Dave flew fish to market.

It was at the height of the summer season with "the land of the midnight sun" expressing itself through long hours of daylight and absence of night. Forty-mile-an-hour winds whipped through our camp situated on a hill overlooking the beach. Temperatures caused Kathy to wear five layers of clothing to preserve body heat. Our high-quality tent was no match for the winds. Time after time, the winds flattened it even though it was secured by metal tubing. Dave ended up building a frame made of two-by-fours inside the tent to withstand the force of constant gales. Miserable conditions compelled cubicle living within the tent much of the time. The ground was still frozen, never completely thawing even in the warmest month of the year. The winds were so strong that one morning we noticed the outhouse was blown some two feet from its moorings of the night before.

Some days were calmer, and the sun beguiled even the most suspicious. On those days, we romped with the girls on the beach in our arctic clothing, searching for antique net buoys. The fishermen were set-netters. That is, they fished by anchoring their nets perpendicular to the shore and extending them 150 feet out into the ocean. Then, when the tide went out, the fishermen extracted the salmon from the nets.

Year after year, the salmon drew fishermen of various sorts to shores throughout the state. Many were commercial fishermen, making their living off the salmon. Others were native Americans who depended on salmon for their subsistence. Still others were sports fishermen who traveled great distances for the excitement salmon fishing offered.

At the camp, Kathy spent most of her days in a tiny canvas cookhouse preparing meals for the fishermen. The cookhouse gave shelter from the elements and provided some semblance of a primitive kitchen. Water for cooking, drinking, dishes, and bathing was taken from a stream a good walk away. Having lived in Africa, Kathy knew the dangers of not boiling water before drinking it. She insisted the water be boiled—and received opposition from the "macho fishermen."

But going into the third week, boiling the water had become an irritation to the fishermen because it was not a convenient process in the crude surroundings. Then, one after another, the men started getting sick. Our kids became ill, and Kathy spent a great deal of time in the outhouse. It was necessary to fly Kathy and the girls back to civilization. Before they left, we discovered that one of the men had short-circuited the steps we took to sterilize the water and had made a packaged drink with untreated water right from the stream. Whether he acted out of ignorance, defiance, or laziness, his actions affected the whole group.

What we do *does* affect those around us. How we spend our money may seem like a personal thing, but especially in marriage that is not the case. The decisions we make can provide happiness and security for those we love, or they can cause conflict and heartache. The underlying personal needs we try to meet through our spending habits often blind us to the more important needs of our families.

There are also certain principles, or laws of nature, if you will, that supersede our desires and actions. If we insist on ignoring those laws, we must accept the resulting consequences. In spending, the parallel remains the same. If we ignore wisdom and overspend or spend selfishly, misuse credit, fail to save, or gamble away our earnings, the subsequent and predictable outcome will diminish our peace, security, and joy of living.

When the winds of crisis strike, a strong inner support system is critical to weathering the storm. If that structure is not in place, we will be like our tent in Alaska. Though it was of high quality, it was not sufficient to withstand the contrary winds of a storm. We must prepare for the difficult times that will surely come by building a structure of strength and stability within our own lives. So much of life revolves around the acquisition, use, or disbursement of money, that we must have an adequate framework to survive the winds of desire and necessity and the multiple voices beckoning us to spend our money.

ATTITUDE CHECK

"The desire to be affluent still motivates much of our activity. . . . Our actions on the job, in the marketplace, with our families and in our free time are greatly impacted by the desire to possess things. Materialism . . . continues to rule the minds and hearts of Americans," says George Barna in *The Frog in the Kettle.*[1]

Melvyn Kinder, in *Going Nowhere Fast,* says, "By focusing so intently on the wishes and fantasies surrounding money we blind ourselves to the negative results that come from its pursuit. We do this partly because the rewards seem so enticing and promising that it all seems worth the effort."[2]

The prevailing attitude in the '80s toward spending was "eat, drink, and be merry, flaunt and spend, for there is no end to what credit will buy." In many families, says Karen O'Connor, in *When Spending Takes the Place of Feeling,* "money was used to manipulate and control, to alter moods, to rescue, to reinforce certain kinds of behavior."[3]

Views on money transcend generations. Kinder notes that "children who are obsessed with designer labels are not merely victims of materialism, they are already conditioned to the very specific signs and symbols of success. There is very little nobility in being poor; there is even less nobility in being out of fashion."[4] Adolescents are

afraid of being different. This mentality continues throughout adult-hood in a culture that encourages peer pressure to fuel the engine of retailing. Without such internal and external pressure working to in-fluence the pocketbooks of the American people, many businesses would no longer exist.

Few possessions can match the level of expectation advertis-ers build into their marketing programs. We are destined for disap-pointment when we believe a product or service can meet deeper emotional needs that can only be filled through relationships.

In an article in *Glamour* magazine, "How Much Money Do You Need to Be Happy?" Pamela Erens argues that obtaining money is not the route to happiness.

> In a study of advanced industrial countries, 72 percent of those in the poorest quarter of the population claimed to be "satisfied" or "very satis-fied" with life as a whole. Among people in the richest quarter, only 14 percent more said the same. But since studies routinely show that it's personal relationships, spirituality and feelings about oneself that most directly influence well-being, those in search of satisfaction would do best to focus on improving these things, not the state of their bank accounts.[5]

Did you ever notice that some of the happiest people are those who have little of this world's goods, and what they do have, they eagerly share? A survey by the Gallup organization concluded that those with lower incomes gave away a greater percentage of their money than those with higher incomes.[6] We have shared a meager meal in an African hut that was bestowed out of delight and sacrifice. It makes us wonder if the joy of giving is not proportional to the personal sacrifice involved in the gift.

If what you really want is to be happy, are you willing to consider that money is only an illusion and mockingly betrays even the most faithful to its pursuit? Does wealth really bring happiness or is happiness through wealth only a mirage that has caused men throughout the ages to waste their lives acquiring things that rotted or were destroyed? Look on the faces of people you see every day. Whose faces are lined with concern and worry; anger and hate; deception and greed; dissatisfaction and disappointment? The wealthy, or the poor? Whose faces reflect peace and security; contentment and joy; courage and perseverance; kindness and compassion? Again, the wealthy, or the poor?

By letting go of our emotional grip on things and the chase for riches, we will free ourselves to more fully enjoy what we do have with a proper perspective. An attitude of gratitude and appreciation is often brought about by a season of deprivation. A few years ago we spent the summer on the French Riviera with our youngest daughter (then twelve years old). Our furnished apartment overlooking a marina on the Mediterranean Sea offered a unique view of a slice of foreign living.

One day we visited an amusement park that featured a high-dive show. The group came from the United States for the summer season. The diver doing the most dangerous dives was introduced as being from the same town in America we lived in. After the show we introduced ourselves and made arrangements for the diver and his wife to join us at our apartment for dinner later in the week.

The young couple had lived in a van previous to their arrival in France in order to save money for airfare. They had little of what many would call necessities. When they came over for dinner, they expressed appreciation in a most refreshing way for even the smallest of gestures. It was encouraging to us, yet at the same time convicting. We realized how much we had come to expect and take for granted. Their gratitude enabled us to rethink our attitudes and abolish minor complaints as they related to our situation in another

culture. A life of plenty can lead to boredom, selfishness, and complacency.

THE BREEZE OF CHANGE

Janice Castro, in an article in *Time* magazine, talks about the
disillusionment Americans have been experiencing over the balanc-
ing act that typifies their lifestyle.

> Because the real weekly wages of average Americans have been falling
> for nearly two decades, most families have staved off downward mobility
> through two costly measures: borrowing money and depending on two
> incomes. In the past year, many people have appraised the results of
> that strategy and decided they have paid a heavy price in their private
> life. With both parents typically holding down a job, home life had been
> reduced to a mad scramble at the end of the day to cram in shopping,
> laundry, cooking, mending—and oh, yes, communication. Adults found they
> had to work harder to hire people to do the work they had not time for.[7]

And they ask themselves, *Is this what living is all about?* We
think not.

The value system of previous decades is under scrutiny, causing good and not so good shifts in our thinking. It used to be that the
number of our possessions was more important than their quality.
Not so anymore. Now people want fewer things but of a higher quality. (But this is not always good, because we can still end up overspending, but in a different capacity.) Also, the value of time is seen
now as worth more than money as a commodity. (Again this change
can be good if we settle for less in the material realm, but bad if we
just work more to earn the money to buy the services we no longer
have the time to perform.) In addition, jobs are no longer seen as
the sole source of satisfaction—leisure is taking its place. (A healthy
slant for workaholics, not so healthy for the unmotivated.)[8]

In the most recent election, many veteran politicians were con-
spicuously absent from the tickets. Even as the government is finally trying to balance the budget by deleting waste and even some
worthwhile projects, constituents and public servants alike are making similar efforts in their personal lives. Reevaluating priorities became the basis of the decision many public servants made to return
to the private sector. By doing so, they could spend more time with
their families and friends instead of with politicians and lobbyists.

CHANGING SPENDING HABITS

It used to be that those who had an abundance of money wanted to let the rest of the world know. In the last few years, the attitude of flaunting wealth has been replaced by the desire to give the impression of humble living. While the riches are still present, the way wealth is expressed has changed. Many are unwilling to continue to appear conspicuous in an era of high unemployment and national economic instability. From not wearing furs, to driving less pretentious automobiles, to not patronizing the poshest restaurants, to hiding their elaborate homes behind tall hedges, the wealthy have made subtle changes in the way they carry out their lives.

On the other hand, those who most want to appear wealthy, but often are not, have an almost unceasing drive to draw attention to their lifestyles. In our world travels we have noticed that the most wealthy are often comfortable in clothing that understates their position in society. It is the person who aspires toward riches who most often tries to give the impression of wealth. They may fool some people, but they never fool themselves. The underlying insecurity that causes them to seek riches is the same insecurity that will keep them from enjoying wealth if it ever comes their way.

Many have sunk themselves deep into debt to keep up the impression that they are wealthy. Not everyone has taken that route, however. Many Americans are waking up to the trumpet sounding the call to let go of the illusion and get out of debt. One writer observes, "Debt is over-extending yourself in order to satisfy some short-term need you have. When you make a commitment to stay out of debt, you are making a commitment to having less than what the world would say you are entitled to."[9]

Janet Castro talks about the changes Americans have made. "In 1991 Americans said, 'Enough.' . . . [They] got back to basics. They cut down on spending, started to pay off their debts and learned to make do with less."[10] That is a significant change. A report from the Consumers Credit Counseling Service indicates that using credit cards increases spending by 34 percent.[11] Robert Powell, in an article in *Your Money,* notes that "everyday spending decisions, especially credit-based decisions, can have a far greater negative impact on your financial future than any investment decision you'll ever make." The emphasis should be on keeping, not earning.[12]

Not all Americans have learned this lesson. Paul Richard notes that "according to *The Wall Street Journal,* 70% of Americans have no money left over after paying basic expenses every month. As food, energy, housing and other costs push higher it makes it more difficult for consumers to keep up, much less get ahead."[13] Nandy Dunnan and Joy J. Pack, in their book *How to Survive and Thrive in the Recession of 1991,* have a similar report. "Unlike the Japanese, who save as much as 25% or more of their income, the average American puts away only about 5% of his or her pre-tax earnings."[14]

One author notes that "there is a way you can have too much money—if you possess it or use it so as to distort more important values and relationships. Furthermore, children as well as adults may be susceptible to this trap."[15] Money itself is not detrimental to living, but the authority we give to it may be.

What we need is to "learn how to accept limits, because they exist, no matter how much money you make," another author asserts. "Acknowledging limits may create a momentary sense of anxiety and sobriety, but when you accept them and learn to live within them, limits actually foster a newfound sense of security. Anxiety thrives on the unknown and the unexpected."[16]

In setting personal limits, make a list of luxuries you are willing to give up in exchange for keeping those that are most important to you. You may be willing to forego your weekly evening out, but not your relaxing hot bath every night. You can easily give up your two-week annual vacation trip in exchange for several shorter and less expensive trips during the year. You don't mind doing without a new couch, but that tattered bedspread has to go. You won't miss the daily newspaper, but your magazine is a favorite. By working within preset boundaries, you will not chafe under the restriction of having to make choices about your spending.

Try to let a month go by without spending money on nonessentials and see if you even notice their absence. We often buy this or that out of habit or impulse, not really caring if we delete it from our lives. Or you might try the 10 percent twist. Decrease the number of trinkets you buy by 10 percent. Be satisfied with 10 percent fewer clothes and accessories. Purchase 10 percent fewer groceries and waste 10 percent less in the refrigerator. Or spend 10 percent less on meals out this month. A 10 percent change results in an almost negligible hardship, yet the savings can add up to a substantial figure.

Enjoyment does not have to be synonymous with ownership. We can enjoy many things that we don't own. Public parks, lakes, museums, beaches, and libraries are for collective enjoyment, not individual ownership. During the summer we lived in southern France, we were invited to the estate of the owner of an airline. Vineyards graced the landscape along the private road into the estate. Acres and acres of beauty surrounded a historical mansion. Some of the finest horses in the country were housed in the stables. The swimming pool overlooked magnificent flower gardens.

In a converted sheep barn, along with other guests we ate from a splendid buffet. Afterward, there was a private recital by a well-known artist. We spent the night in a separate guest house that made you feel as though you were living in another century. Yes, we enjoyed our stay. No, we had no desire to own what we were enjoying. We were content to just appreciate our time with our host and his wife, and to take pleasure in their good fortune.

We have enjoyed special times with others in their boats, airplanes, and mountain cabins, never feeling as though we needed or wanted to own what they possessed, yet allowing ourselves to delight in sharing it with them. When we were in Acapulco, a billionaire invited us to his birthday party. His unusual home sat high on the cliffs above the ocean. On the warm, starlit night we descended the path to the lower swimming pool close to the beach. Strains from the private orchestra gave the evening a romantic appeal. Up above, there was another pool with separate guest houses in an exotic setting. The linen, crystal, china, silver, waiters, and fine delicacies all blended to make a very special evening. There was enjoyment, but not covetousness. We were free to appreciate without the desire to possess what another owned.

What about you? Maybe you will never have similar opportunities, but are you enjoying what you do have and not longing for what you don't? Do you appreciate the times you share with others, whether what they have is meager or abundant? And they with you?

Are you buying "things" beyond what is necessary for simple enjoyment? Before making a purchase, consider your spouse's feelings. Is he or she in agreement, and will the purchase contribute to the family's happiness, unity, and harmony? Is the item essential? If it is, would a less expensive model serve the same purpose? Do you have the money to spare? Or could the money be better spent on something that meets a higher priority? What additional upkeep in cost or time will it require? Do you lean toward excess to make a visual impression on others? How does spending money make you feel? To help us explore alternatives to traditional buying habits, consider these options.

OPTIONS COMING OF AGE

Mortgage Buster

In this era of fluctuating interest rates, a wise investment is to pay off your mortgage early. In our case, in six years we can pay off the house we purchased last year by making one additional principle payment a month, rather than paying almost two hundred thousand dollars additional interest over the thirty-year loan period. (And this is on a modest home. Think what the savings would be on a higher-priced house.) This extra payment does not include taxes and insurance, so it is less than a double house payment. Our loan is at 9 percent and we plan on staying in the home for quite some time. The rate of return on a low-risk investment such as this would be hard to beat in today's economy. Even an additional payment of one hundred dollars a month will drastically reduce the interest you will pay over the life of your loan by many thousands of dollars.

"Some [financial] planners recommend that you try to increase your net worth—the value of what you own minus the value of what you owe—by about ten percent per year," Robert Powell reports.[17] With the aging of the baby boomers, their flagrant spending habits are being replaced by more reasonable pursuits—paying for their children's college or planning for retirement. In fact, Joe Urschel of *USA Today* claims the boomers' will to shop is spent, and they "are looking at the rungs above them," only to find that "they are clogged with other boomers. . . . Meanwhile companies are downsizing. Welcome to promotional gridlock in the land where success means keeping your job, and the lucky few get raises that beat inflation."[18]

And the tax bite gets more painful. "Federal, state and local taxes will together absorb almost 40 percent of a typical American family's budget in 1992—more than food, clothing and housing combined," an article in *The Reader's Digest* reported.[19]

Negotiate!

Negotiating is quickly becoming the norm for items once considered unnegotiable. It is no longer considered cheap, but rather smart, to ask for the best price a vendor can give you. "Haggling has never been much of a tradition in the U.S., the way it is in some parts of the world," writes Jeffrey A. Trachtenberg in an article on demanding and getting discounts. "Though American shoppers have always kept a sharp eye out for sales," Trachtenberg continues,

> they have generally expected to have to pay the ticketed price, whether buying furniture, clothes, or TV sets. But now, the recession has battered demand so much that this is beginning to change. Consumers are sensing the clout they have when they walk into half-empty stores. And more and more are cranking up their courage and asking the seller if he "can do a little better." Call it the new price gap—the difference between what manufactures and retailers ask for their goods and what today's consumers will pay.[20]

Jere Daniel, writing in *Family Circle* magazine, agrees with Trachtenberg's assessment of the new attitude. "Though we know enough to bargain on cars and houses, we skip the opportunity to knock down the price in a store—perhaps by 25% to 40%—because we don't realize how willing merchants are to bargain."[21] It is important to comparison shop and gather relevant product information before making an offer. Determine what features you would like, what you are willing to pay, and the competition's prices. Then with confidence approach someone who has the authority to give you a better deal. Time your shopping trip to take advantage of salesmen trying to meet end-of-the-month quotas. They should be more willing to give you a better price.

Try to shop during the slow time of day or week when you can speak with the manager personally, and when your good fortune will not be jeopardized by the presence of other customers. Your leverage increases the higher the ticket price and the greater the quantity you wish to purchase. By buying two or three high-priced items (that you have deemed necessary and that are in your budget), you can usually be successful in obtaining an even greater discount than if the items were bought separately. "Negotiation experts advise you to be willing not to buy something if you don't feel the price is right," Daniel says. "Sometimes, they say, you have to chance saying no. . . . Be prepared not to get it; but don't be too surprised if you get a phone call and an offer a few days later. . . . When it comes to negotiating, keep in mind that very often good things come to those who wait."[22]

When the drip on our kitchen faucet became a steady stream, Dave took the thirty-year-old fixture apart to change a washer. Iron-dense water had built up rust on the fixture's inner workings and not only could it not be repaired, Dave couldn't even separate the pieces from one another. It was during a season of unemployment and we did not need another surprise expenditure. Having no choice but to track down a replacement if we wanted to use the kitchen sink, Dave was unsuccessful in locating a used faucet. Scouring the town for the best price on new models he found that the prices ranged from $40 to $215. Surprised at the substantial difference in prices, he asked one clerk how it could be. It seems the lower-priced offerings were made of plastic and painted with a chrome or gold finish to look like metal.

Then in one store Dave found a display model with special features marked at $195.00 He noticed that it was a discontinued design. Dave asked the clerk if he would take $60.00 for it. The response was that the merchant would sell it for $75.00. So Dave left and continued looking elsewhere. Then he returned an hour later to reconsider the display model. It was then that Dave realized the merchant probably hadn't had to purchase the unit because it was a manufacturer's display, and since it was discontinued, he probably couldn't sell it for the full price. Dave took the unit to the front and said, "Are you sure you can't take sixty dollars?" This time the reply was, "OK, I'll split the difference." So Dave bought a $195.00 solid brass fixture for $67.50.

Earlier this week we went as a family to cut our Christmas tree. After having a grand time selecting just the "right" tree we noticed tree stands that were for sale. Every year Dave spends much time and frustration trying to come up with a contraption that actually works in lieu of buying a stand. But these looked solid, so Dave asked if the owner would take two dollars off the price. No problem. (It gets easier all the time!)

We are finding that all you have to do is ask, and most merchants are willing to oblige just to make a sale. Of course, as in Mexico where haggling is a way of life, people are insulted if you offer them too low a price. In any negotiations, first discover what it is the other person wants. Perhaps what he or she is asking for is only one way to meet their real need.

For example, suppose one of your teenagers approaches you about doing odd jobs around the house. You do have some work you have been putting off that would be just the thing for the teen. But you are low on cash. After finding out that the teen wants to earn money to buy a minibike you remember that you have one you haven't used for two years stashed in the garage. Aha! You make a deal. So many hours of work in exchange for the minibike. You get what you want, the teen gets what he or she wants, and you don't have to spend any money in the process.

Recognize and try to match another's negotiating style. If you come across like a bulldozer to a gentle-spirited sort, you may never get beyond the person's fear of intimidation. On the other hand, if you persist in exchanging small talk and the other person enjoys being direct, you may frustrate them to the point of being unwilling to negotiate.

Service Contracts

Warranties on products are usually covered in the price of the product, whereas extended service contracts are an additional expense. Service contracts are often written to benefit the seller rather than the buyer and sometimes duplicate the warranty. It may be more feasible to pay for repairs than to pay for this coverage. Find out how often you would realistically need the service and if it is really worth the cost.

Returning Merchandise

As consumers, we are not bound by a purchase if the product does not fulfill advertising claims or if we change our minds. Most stores have generous return policies. Keep your receipts and get to know the policies at the stores you patronize the most. Maybe when you get an item home it doesn't match the way you thought it would. Or after second thought you realize you really shouldn't have spent the money (or maybe your spouse thinks you shouldn't have). If the item is not damaged or used, and was not purchased on a closeout sale, then you should have great latitude in taking it back. What this does is give the consumer (especially an impulsive one) an out if he is just learning to control his spending and isn't always successful. Or maybe when you get something home you realize right away it will not satisfy the emotional need you thought it would. Take it back —there is no disgrace in changing your mind. Just be truthful, polite, and speak to the manager if necessary.

Returning inferior merchandise makes the manufacture accountable for honesty in advertising and maintaining product quality. "Call for Action," 3400 Idaho Ave. N.W., Suite 101, Washington, D.C. 20016; (202) 537-0585, is a resource that may be of help if you feel you have been shortchanged through fraudulent advertising or inflated charges. Contact them for an affiliate hot line nearest you if you are having difficulty receiving a refund or follow-through on a warranty or guarantee.

Joint Ownership

Joint ownership is making a comeback. It's the scenario that takes place when you buy a small boat, your neighbor buys the motor, you both share other expenses (marina fees, upkeep, and so on), and you both enjoy an activity you might otherwise never have experienced. The concept of joint ownership irritates the independent spirit we as Americans have embraced. A sense of community and accountability is sometimes seen as an impertinent intrusion into our fast-track lifestyle. By overcoming the tendency to glorify individuality, we may find joint ownership a feasible option.

Bartering

In primitive cultures, bartering is much more natural than in ours. A machete in exchange for manioc. Cows for a bride. Cloth for rice. Baskets for meat. Carvings for palm oil. In our country, the shyness is wearing off. Corporations and individual consumers alike are learning the intricacies of trade without cash. If you have a lawn-care business and need some roof work done, by trading services with a roofer, both of you will benefit by not having to come up with cash. The catch is that the value of the bartered goods is taxed by the IRS. The system works best if you only trade for what you would buy anyway. You own a carpet store and need a new refriger-

ator. You find that an appliance dealer in town is checking out carpeting for his remodeling project. By making an equitable trade, you
both save.

Susan Karlin, writing for the *Los Angeles Times,* says of bartering, "It wasn't until 30 years ago that bartering became an industry,
after the advent of small computers made it possible to cheaply track
many transactions involving different parties at different times. During the past decade, the business has grown from $200 million a year
to $1 billion."[23] There are bartering associations that match up ser-
vices, products, and businesses. If you send a self-addressed,
stamped envelope to the International Reciprocal Trade Association, 9513 Beach Mill Rd. Great Falls, VA 22066, the association
will send you more information about bartering and a list of barter
exchanges near you.

Auctions

Auctions can either be a vice or a virtue when it comes to saving money. If you are looking for a special touch to your home, you
might be able to buy a unique piece of furniture for only five dollars.
Or if you just need some basics but hate to spend the money for new
items, an auction may be just the thing. When we first moved to this
location, we needed some outdoor tools. Our first auction in many
years was to be more of a special event than a shopping trip. Dave
was listening to the goings-on in a barn while Kathy was taking in
the items being sold outside. Being new to the auction game, Kathy
made a bid on a pair of axes (or so she thought) for Dave to use in
his yard work. The auctioneer was holding up the axes together and
was talking fast. The bid was at three dollars. Kathy raised it to four
dollars without a higher bid to follow. Kathy thought she did quite
well until she was told that they were four dollars *each.* Somewhere
she missed something. That same day we bought a vacuum cleaner for
three dollars since ours had recently died. One man bought a wheel-
barrow for two dollars. When Dave offered him three dollars for it,
the farmer was eager to accept, since he had only bought the wheel-
barrow to transfer all his finds from the auction site to his truck.

But we also noticed something else about auctions. People
could easily pay more for a used item than what they would pay for a
new one at a store. It is important to research the price of items you

are in the market for, set your limit in writing, and not go beyond it, even in the emotional atmosphere created specifically to encourage you to do so. Several months ago the washing machine that came with this house quit. Dave took it apart only to find that the cost of replacement parts would be more than the cost of a newer model. After checking the papers for an upcoming auction that featured a washing machine, we made plans to attend that weekend. When the washing machine finally came up for bid, we had already agreed on a limit. We were both amazed at the final bid. Someone sure didn't do his homework.

We once bought a car at an auction and saved hundreds of dollars. There are real estate, jewelry, and boat auctions; bankruptcy, government, and estate auctions. The best place to find out what's going on in your area is to investigate the classified ads.

Outlet Malls

With consumers becoming more conscious of value and less driven by fads and fancies, outlet malls have surged to the forefront. Name-brand clothing, tableware, toys, and hardware are popular items featured in these price-slashing ventures. Manufacturers are passing over middlemen and going directly to the customers. There are over 8,000 outlet stores in more than 300 designated malls. For information or free brochures on outlet centers in your area or near a planned vacation site, write to: Outletbound, P.O. Box 1255-D, Orange, CT 06477; or call (800) 336-8853.

In any spending you undertake, have a plan. If you know you are an impulsive individual, work that into your plan, allotting a portion of your budget for that tendency. Learn to restrict yourself and not extend beyond that limit. If you are trying to meet unfulfilled needs, or if you know your spending habits are out of line, an excellent resource for additional insight and help is a book mentioned earlier: Karen O'Connor, *When Spending Takes the Place of Feeling* (Nashville: Thomas Nelson, 1992). Spending doesn't satisfy our deepest needs. But stay tuned. We'll show you what really does satisfy in a later chapter.

NOTES

1. George Barna, *The Frog in The Kettle: What Christians Need to Know About Life in the Year 2000* (Ventura, Calif.: Regal, 1990), 33.

2. Melvyn Kinder, *Going Nowhere Fast: Step Off Life's Treadmills and Find Peace of Mind* (New York: Fawcett Columbine, 1990), 84.

3. Karen O'Connor, *When Spending Takes the Place of Feeling* (Nashville: Thomas Nelson, 1992), 23.

4. Kinder, 86.

5. Pamela Erens, "How Much Money Do You Need to Be Happy?" *Glamour,* June 1992, 44. Erens is quoting David G. Myers, *The Pursuit of Happiness: What Makes a Person Happy—And Why* (New York: William Morrow, 1992).

6. Pamela Sebastian, "Recession Hurts Giving of Cash, Not Volunteering," *The Wall Street Journal,* 15 October 1992, 86B.

7. Janice Castro, "The New Frugality," *Time,* 6 January 1992, 41.

8. Barna, 33.

9. Ron Blue, "Managing Your Money Better," *Today's Better Life,* Summer 1992.

10. Castro, "The New Frugality," 41.

11. O'Connor, 87.

12. Robert Powell, "How You Can Become Financially Secure," *Your Money* 13, no. 6 (October/November 1992), 15.

13. Paul Richard, "21 Tips for Wiser Holiday Spending," National Center for Financial Education news release, November 1992, p. 1.

14. Nancy Dunnan and Jay J. Pack, *How to Survive and Thrive in the Recession of 1991* (New York: Avon, 1991), 21.

15. Ralph E. Minear and William Proctor, *Kids Who Have Too Much* (Nashville: Thomas Nelson, 1989), 93.

16. Kinder, 99.

17. Powell, "How You Can Become Financially Secure," 16.

18. Joe Urschel, "Boomers No Longer Fuel Boom," *USA Today,* 7 May 1992, editorial page.

19. "Where Does the Family Dollar Go" [Condensed from *Reason*], *Reader's Digest,* September 1992, 75.

20. Jeffrey A. Trachtenberg, "Let's Make a Deal; A Buyer's Market Has Shoppers Demanding And Getting Discounts," *The Wall Street Journal,* 8 February 1991, 1.

21. Dan Moreau, "5 Rules For Happy Haggling," *Changing Times,* April 1991, 59.

22. Jere Daniel, "Talk Your Way to a Good Deal," *Family Circle,* 7 January 1992, 37.

23. Susan Karlin, "Bartering Can Offer an Edge in Difficult Times," *Los Angeles Times,* 29 November 1991, D6.

Activities
for Sale

PART 5

13

Motion Mentality

Three hundred feared dead in a freak flash flood last night in Rapid City, South Dakota!" The radio announcer's voice cut into the programming on the car radio. We were on our way from Chicago to Alaska to spend the summer working at a camp. Jeannette was only a year old and the other two girls had not yet been born.

We were expected to be at the camp for orientation on a certain date. We needed to allow for ten days to make the four thousand-mile trip, including more than twelve hundred of them on gravel road. However, the camp director wrote and asked us to be there a few days earlier than planned. Wrapping up arrangements in Chicago brought one unexpected delay after another. Frustration mounted as the departure day drew nearer. In the end, no matter how hard we tried, we were prevented from leaving on the specified date. It made no sense. Obstacles from nowhere appeared almost deliberately and thwarted our plans. We left twenty-four hours later than intended.

"Rapid City. Is that anywhere near here?" Kathy quizzed Dave, trying to find their location on the map. We realized that we had camped only three hundred miles from Rapid City the night before. All of the radio stations were now dedicated to reporting the chaos and rescue efforts. Disbelief and a twinge of panic came through the usually controlled voices of DJs. Most of the deaths had occurred in a campground in a valley. Apparently, with widespread rain, an overswollen dam at the top of a ravine burst, causing a succession of dams to break on the river's downward path of destruction that engulfed the valley below.

Then it dawned on us. That was the very area in which we had planned on camping. Had we left a day earlier, we might have been among those washed away by the torrent of death. We were so intent on fulfilling "our plans" that we were not still enough to sense God's leading in our departure date. Throughout the morning, as we listened spellbound to the accounts of the tragedy of the night before, we experienced a sense of God's protection and presence in a new way.

How often we need to be reminded that as we rush through life we may be jeopardizing our very lives, not only in the physical sense but also in the emotional and relational sense. We ignore our health because we are too busy; we repress happiness as well as disappointment because we have no time to fully enjoy or work through those emotions; we give up on relationships because they require too much of ourselves, both in time and energy.

The writer of a CBS news special, "48 Hours in Time," had this to say concerning the pace of life today: "In 1990 we will have more people to meet, more things to do, and more money to spend than our grandparents had in their lifetimes. . . . After 15 seconds of waiting in fast food lines, horns begin to blow in the drive-thru. . . . The human race is living up to its name."[1] And what is it all for? Is it just a neurotic striving for meaning fueled by fear, emptiness, desire, and greed? Or is it complacency and apathy, allowing ourselves to be swept along by the status quo, embracing inferior values and perspectives? Or could it be an escape from facing ourselves, our pain, our past, our weaknesses, or our future?

Kathy remembers reading the following anonymous poem over the loudspeaker in high school on one of the mornings she was slated to give the announcements.

Tomorrow

He was going to be all that a mortal should be—Tomorrow.
No one should be kinder or braver than he—Tomorrow.
A friend who was troubled and weary he knew,
Who'd be glad of a lift and who needed it too;
On him he would call and see what he could do—Tomorrow.

Each morning he stacked up the letters he'd write—Tomorrow.
And thought of the folks he would fill with delight—Tomorrow.
It was too bad, indeed, he was busy today,
And hadn't a minute to stop on his way;
More time he would have to give others, he'd say—Tomorrow.
The greatest of workers he would have been—Tomorrow.
The world would have known him had he ever seen Tomorrow.
But the fact is, he died and faded from view
And all he left when living was through
Was a mountain of things he intended to do—Tomorrow.

Yes, Americans are busier than ever, but at what price? Do those most meaningful and important tasks ever get done in the scurry for the frivolous and superficial? Most of us are aware of the devastation that trying to meet the constant drone of demands can bring to otherwise normal people.

Sure, it may be fun to whittle our time away on empty pursuits (the makings of future regrets); and it probably is exciting to be caught up in a frenzied pace (for a while); and it does makes us feel important for others to ask us to be on this committee or head that project (until we drop from exhaustion). It is only as we relate each activity to our central purpose for living that can we undertake an intelligent selection process.

In our upbeat society we have been trained to accept terse and sporadic attention spans as the norm. The media, technological advancement, and laziness have spurred us on to greater heights in our demand for entertainment as an occupation.

Coupled with mass insecurity that directly feeds the pockets of unscrupulous advertisers, the stage has been set for nonstop activity. Because so many people are afraid to get to know and accept themselves, speeding up life helps them to deaden the ache, avoid facing reality, and increase their sense of self-importance.

Opportunities are more valued and appreciated if they don't have to compete with other activities until life becomes a burden. When we are overcommitted we start to resent any demands on our time, even the most important ones involving our families.

Do your children have adequate intervals for just being children? Come with us a moment as we review a childhood memory of Kathy's that would not have been possible if her parents had scheduled a continuous round of activities for her while she was growing up.

It has been many years since I visited my parents' home in Pennsylvania. Our worldwide travels have left few opportunities for such a trek. My parents' large yard doesn't seem large any more. In fact, it seems quiet small compared to vastness once seen through a child's eyes. The daffodils still bloom at the side of the house. Their new beginning each spring lent a flavor of freshness and excitement to life—and signaled that school was drawing to a close for the year.

Today as I rounded the corner of the house to visit my beloved apple tree, my heart wrenched with sadness when empty ground greeted me where once had stood a special friend. Through three seasons of each year, its leaves would hide me from the rest of the world. What joy it was to spend hours in its branches, where I could soar to heights in my imagination and no one could hinder me. There, looking down on another domain, I would analyze, contemplate, ponder, dream, think, wonder, and strain my brain to find the answers to questions not yet formed. I was driven to use my mind; to push it beyond the status quo; to grasp, to grope, to reach.

The varying moods of morning freshness, afternoon intensity, and evening restfulness—all predictable, yet each unique—changed as the sun's path moved ever so slightly from day to day throughout the seasons. Shaded by the gnarled, protective arms of the apple tree was an even more significant friend that helped me experience childhood. My confidant was a playhouse measuring only three feet by four feet of inside floor space.

Usually Dad made most of our playthings for us: the tree house, the bag swing out over the hill, the cable ride from our tree house to the swimming pool, the wooden diving board, makeshift tents over old swing set frames, the sandbox, a miniature racetrack complete with a miniature car that pulled a handmade trailer for extra passengers, scarecrows, kid-sized garden plots . . .

But this was a commercial playhouse with tiny windows outlined by authentic shutters. The red and white exterior was accented by window boxes where we lovingly planted real flowers each spring. The gabled-shingled roof over a sturdy body extended itself to allow for a petite porch held securely with stately white columns. Our playhouse sat regally year after year under a covering of shade from the old apple tree.

Inside there was a built-in cupboard that graced the entire three feet of height. It was ideal for our miniature dishes and play foods. Many a real peanut butter and jelly sandwich were enjoyed as I sat cross-legged in the middle of the floor. In the playhouse I decorated, furnished, cooked, cleaned with a tiny broom, dusted, mopped, and scrubbed with real soap and water. Even though the playhouse belonged to my three sisters as well, I was its undisputed mistress (at least in my own mind). It became my first home.

It was my friend long after the others lost interest. Even now, tears threaten to emerge when I remember the fondness I had had for my companion. How hard it became for me to squeeze through the wee entrance as my body kept growing beyond my desire to give up my home. Inside, I had to sit scrunched up with my knees to my chest. No longer did I move about my home with freedom. The linoleum floor was cracked and graying. The cupboard door was askew on its hinges. When I gazed out of the dainty windows, I could see peeled and discolored paint on the shutters. The overhang that was once a porch rested precariously on one unstable stick of wood, the stately columns long ago discarded.

As adolescence descended, how I wished I could have reversed the playhouse's aging. I felt helpless and despondent, longing for what could never be again. There would be no more pretending.

Gone were innocent dreams once cherished. The security of the familiar gave way to the tumult of teenage years. A friend sat dying —and I was growing up. Now, many years later, those memories skip through my heart with sadness bathed in an almost forgotten joy. They call it bittersweet. I wonder how much of what I am today was influenced by those early experiences.

What kind of experiences are you allowing your children? Will they look back on their childhoods and remember only busyness with no time for reflection and inner growth? Will they sense that all those activities were just a tactic to give you more time to yourself? Will they resent the pressure you have placed on them to perform, compete, and excel so that you could vicariously live through them?

And what about your own schedule? Do you regularly plan high stress activities back-to-back with no time to recharge your batteries? Do you allow yourself to be talked into attending useless meetings because you fear rejection? Do you give yourself at least twenty-four hours to consider accepting leadership positions and then evaluate your decision based on your current commitments, life goals, and personal desires?

One couple decided that the cost of busyness was too expensive. "Addicted to our own adrenaline, we sprinted from one meeting to the next, one more appointment, one more deadline, saying, 'If we can just hang on until things slow down, maybe in March, or April . . .' But March and April had their own expectations, and we always postponed that break in the action a few more weeks. Always a few more weeks. Always hanging in there until next time."[2]

The couple's lifestyle was part of the expected middle-class American treadmill. "It was a busy morning. But busy was good. Life didn't seem to count unless I functioned at a roller coaster pace. Busyness meant that I counted for something, that I was being mature, holding up my part, being responsible. All I had to do was say I was busy and people would nod their heads knowingly. 'How are you? Busy? Good, good.' It was an old conversation."[3]

Chaotic living in a world that often makes no sense contributes to emptiness, desperation, and broken relationships. "What a price we pay for the speed at which we run!" James Dobson says.

Already, the new year we greeted last January has dwindled to its twilight hours. It will soon recede into history. Most of us remember those last 12 months as a blur of activity. There was so much work to do. There were so many demands on our time. There was so much pressure.

Meanwhile, what should have mattered most was often put on hold—or shortchanged or ignored altogether. Millions of children received very little love and guidance this year from their busy parents. Husbands and wives passed like ships in the night.[4]

We treat our busyness with such indifference that it seems we are blinded to the severe consequences of excessiveness in scheduling. There is a price to pay, the Family Research Council says: "A 1989 survey commissioned by the Massachusetts Mutual Insurance Company found that Americans believe 'Parents having less time to spend with their families' is the single most important reason for the family's decline in our society."[5]

Hurried children are an outgrowth of the busyness mentality. David Elkin argues that "hurried children grow up too fast, pushed in their early years toward many different types of achievement and exposed to experiences that tax their adaptive capacity. . . . Hurried children are stressed by the fear of failure—of not achieving fast enough or high enough. [They] are forced to take on the physical, psychological, and social trappings of adulthood before they are prepared to deal with them."[6]

Date books overrun with incessant activity take a toll on physical health. When our health begins to unravel, living loses its zest and deteriorates into reluctant participation in endurance. "Many doctors believe that life has become so hectic in the past 25 years that our bodies are in stressful states most of the time," says Jan Markel in *Overcoming Stress*.[7] The seventh most common health complaint today is chronic fatigue, a syndrome one writer describes as "a down-to-the-bones, debilitating fatigue that lingers for weeks and may be a prelude to a host of other health complaints."[8]

One author shares a glimpse of what propelled him to live precariously beyond logic or sensibility. "All the running hadn't accomplished anything except to make my life miserable and me not much fun to live with. Rush, rush, rush. Hurry, Hurry, hurry. And for what? To be honest, I would have to say, 'Because it made me feel important.' Important people always rush. Having no time was a status symbol."⁹ Complicated lifestyles induce a false sense of significance.

Boredom is often synonymous with dullness. But actually boredom and its counterpart, idleness, can be quite beneficial. Boredom stimulates creativity in an effort to relieve anxiety. For our own children, the times when they were the most bored were also some of the times when their artistic, sewing, baking, or decorating talents were most evident. Idleness allows for time to think, relax, and appreciate.

Occasional periods of solitude to evaluate one's life differs from a classic symptom of burnout—detachment. Burnout causes you to withdraw from exhaustion, and often stimulates an attitude of cynicism, resentment, and irritability. In contrast, intervals of voluntary seclusion actually help to prevent burnout from occurring.

But to some, silence is deafening. They prefer to fill space with noise. To others, silence brings reminders of failure, grief, or betrayal. And to still others, silence is a source of strength that puts all of life into proper perspective.

We are uncomfortable with boredom because our society has dictated a marriage of activity and usefulness. It has condoned passive, vicarious existence in place of active, vibrant living. Although being caught up in activity may masquerade as usefulness, in reality, if one has not predetermined his or her purpose in life, activity is only a cover-up. Usually it takes a season of solitude to determine our purpose and then regular checkups to see if we are still on track. It is difficult to do either during the daily drama of living.

"Most of us live to a staccato beat, pulled and jerked from one role to another," says Gloria Gaither. "I have come to believe that one of the crying needs in me and in our culture is the need for silence and solitude."¹⁰

But how is this possible in today's society? One writer observes, "Increasingly, family schedules are intricate applications of time-motion principles, with everything engineered to the minute and with every piece designed to fall in the right place at the right time."¹¹

In time, frustration occurs at the deepest level causing an inner resolve to recapture a sense of control and calm. In *'Tis a Gift to Be Simple,* one of the authors says: "This wind-up-toy life-style demanded I march to its pace. I wanted my life back. I knew it would mean changing something, even some big things, but I was determined to find a different pace for this marathon called life that would leave me with breath at the finish line."[12]

In the primitive societies of Africa, time is measured by passing generations, recurring seasons, and the immutable predictability of the sun. The perpetual cycles of birth and death provide the threads that weave whole cultures together. The hustle and bustle of overloaded schedules is unknown. There is continuity and a sense of tranquillity as the Africans plow their gardens and try to eke out an existence. You would think that with all of our advantages and conveniences we would be unimpeded from living at a slower pace.

But that is not the case. In our society it takes a conscious effort to slow down, and when we do slow down our choice is often misunderstood, condemned, or ridiculed. The authors of *'Tis a Gift to Be Simple* describe the way they managed the exodus out of the fast lane:

> Step one was to free ourselves of some of that cumbersome load. We put our house on the market. We reduced our job commitments by half. We cut other things in half: mortgage, taxes, house size. A drastic move? Yes. A bit hasty? Perhaps. But it allowed us the energy to breathe easy once again.
>
> There were withdrawal symptoms. Old habits are hard to break. Old voices continued to scream, "Hurry up! No one moves down. Up is the way to go. Up, up, up. More, more, more." But slowly we gained the needed space to reflect. We played more with our children. We filled the void with good books and conversation. We still had some frantic nights when everyone needed to be somewhere at the same time but far fewer than before. In the quiet moments we began to find value in important things we once labeled a waste of time.[13]

Have you ever noticed when there is an accident on the freeway, everyone instinctively slows down, whether out of curiosity or because of the immediate hazard? For some miles afterward, drivers seem to lose their sense of urgency to get somewhere fast. Perhaps they experience a season of reflection. *That could have been me. Have I done all I could to make the most of the relationships nearest to me? No, there are some things I need to make right before I die. I'll have to do that the first chance I get.* Then, in the drone of monotonous miles, those thoughts fade, the wheels pick up speed, and life continues as usual. Rarely do we make good on those fleeting thoughts as the immediate screams for attention amid a life of constant movement. The next chapter will show you how to escape the whirlwind of activity, allowing the emphasis of your life to focus on relationships and on finding the satisfaction erroneously sought through unending motion.

NOTES

1. CBS News Special, "48 Hours in Time," 8 March 1990.

2. Reprinted by permission from *'Tis a Gift to Be Simple* by Barbara DeGrotte-Sorenson and David Allen Sorenson, copyright © Augsburg Fortress, 2.

3. Ibid., 3.

4. James C. Dobson, Focus on the Family Newsletter, December 1992, 1.

5. Family Research Council, "Family Time: What Americans Want" *In Focus*, Gary Bauer, editor, February, 1991, 1.

6. David Elkind, *The Hurried Child: Growing Up Too Fast Too Soon* (Reading, Mass.: Addison-Wesley, 1981), xii.

7. Jan Markell, *Overcoming Stress* (Wheaton, Ill.: Victor, 1982).

8. Karen Edmonds, "Chronic Fatigue Syndrome," *Sunshine Horizons*, August/September 1992, 8.

9. DeGrotte-Sorenson and Sorenson, 4.

10. Gloria Gaither, "When Silence Comes," *Virtue* (October 1988), 15.

11. Barbara Whitehead as quoted by William R. Mattox, Jr., "The Parent Trap, So Many Bills, So Little Time," *Policy Review* (Winter, 1991), 6.

12. DeGrotte-Sorenson and Sorenson, 4.

13. Ibid., 8–9.

14

Activities: Fun or Frenzy?

Before arriving in Africa, we had heard glowing reports about how magnificent a city Nairobi, Kenya, was, and we looked forward to seeing it. It was to be the last city we would see before we took a small plane to the northeast corner of Zaire. But when we arrived in Nairobi we were disappointed at the endorsement it had received. By American standards, the city was primitive and dirty.

After living in the interior of Zaire for over a year, we had an opportunity to take a "real" vacation on the Indian Ocean. The same small plane that had taken us into the jungle of Zaire would return us to Nairobi, where we were to catch a train south to Mombasa for a week's stay on the coast. This time, when we arrived in Nairobi we were jolted with how wonderful the city was. How our perspective had changed in the past months. When we were overloaded on what America had to offer, an inferior city paled in comparison. But take us away from progressive civilization for a year and a new sense of appreciation dawns.

As we continued on to Mombasa, excitement prevailed for our whole family. The resort where we had booked reservations had individual (modernized) African huts with grass thatched roofs. We had reserved one for the girls and one for us. After a long train ride we arrived to inhale the beauty of the Indian Ocean that promised to make this a special vacation indeed.

All of the meals were included in the vacation package. In a large, open, grass-covered structure, meals were served buffet style. The first morning we were astonished at the feast that awaited us. There were fresh fruits, baked delicacies, all kinds of meat and egg entrees, juices, and exotic offerings that charmed starved travelers.

We ate and ate, filling ourselves with a selection of foods we couldn't even have imagined a week earlier. Frolicking in the warm currents of a clear, blue-green ocean that morning was a delight for each of us. Then we feasted at the lunch buffet—an array of specialities laid out with creativity and class. There seemed to be no end to our appetite for such fine food. Dinner featured candlelight, warm breezes, soft music, and more lavish, mouth-watering choices.

The first two days we spent an excessive amount of time dining and enjoying the rich display set before us. After about the third day, we noticed that we started to eat less at each meal. We still enjoyed the fare immensely, however. By the fifth day, we were quite satiated and even began to skip the afternoon meal. No longer did we awaken with excitement about the day's culinary offerings enticing us toward the ocean's edge. We had begun to take the bounty for granted. We had reached our fill. We had gorged ourselves until there was no hunger left. That first thrill over the menu had mellowed into complacency. Although we had never had a healthier diet than when we were in Zaire, the enticement of variety was overwhelming.

There is a parallel to our dining experience in the frenzied lifestyle of most Americans. The first thrill of participation eventually mellows into complacency. We so indulge ourselves with the bounty of choice, that we become overloaded and fail to enjoy life with the same intensity as before. For some, no enjoyment is left at all. Your current diet of activities may be bland, but you might be overwhelmed at an overabundnce of variety. Discipline and wisdom are imperative to maintaining a balanced life.

Think about the typical American family. Brad is in corporate middle management a thirty-mintue commute away. Counting his travel time he is gone from home eleven or twelve hours a day. In addition, he works some Saturdays and often brings projects home in the evening. His wife, Katie, has a part-time position as a receptionist in a doctor's office. She has arranged her working hours so

that she can be home when the children arrive from school. It's a good thing, too, because barely does her workday end when her shift as chauffeur begins.

In a typical week son Jim, fifteen, has two basketball games to play in addition to practices after school. The whole family tries to go to the home games. But lately it has become a juggling act for even one of them to be there to root for Jim. On weekends Jim works for a builder doing odd jobs. He has had to drop out of band because the requirements conflicted with basketball. He has also had give up any hope of a part in the school play. Special school activities give him some semblance of social life.

Susan, twelve, has been taking gymnastics since she was a toddler. As her proficiency increased, so did the number of practices and meets. Of course Brad and Katie want to be spectators as often as they can. When Susan is not at gymnastics, she is trying to fit in her piano lessons and practice time, or she is auditioning for bit parts in commercials. Baby-sitting opportunities are emerging more frequently as she proves her dependability with young mothers in the neighborhood.

And Joey, eight, is just beginning to discover the wonderful possibilities in store for him. He is on a junior swim team, with practice three times a week and meets at least once a week. With school in full-swing, Joey is often invited to get involved in scouting, band, or a community fund-raising project for kids.

Katie sees her mother role as one of keeping the home running smoothly and manipulating the daily schedule so that everyone arrives at his or her respective destination on time. Often Katie has to recruit a double to chauffeur her children from one activity or another. Family meals together have become a rarity. Nerves fray as minutes between activities dwindle. Homework is relegated to the bottom of the list. There is just no time or energy. And now Brad is required to put in even more hours at work because his corporation recently downsized and eliminated hundreds of workers. Those who survived the cut are expected to take up the slack.

Katie tries to work in fun times for herself. Aside from weekly trips to the grocery store and mall, she takes an evening art class, tries to make crafts for the local craft fair, exercises with an early-morning aerobics class, and enjoys lunch with friends. She also welcomes going to the library, taking in a movie one night a week with Brad, and serving on community projects from time to time.

The Martins used to go to church and participate in various groups but lately church seems to have been the one variable easy to drop. Sometimes the Martins feel as though they are being pulled by wants, shoulds, and musts. Juggling it all is becoming a nightmare as energy levels drop, tempers flare, and misunderstandings occur more frequently. There is just no time to sit down and work out reasonable solutions or improve the level of communication between family members. Besides, each has his own hassles in his world of work or school. No one needs additional ones at home.

The Martins' dilemma is being played out in homes all across America. When single parenting is added to the mix, managing it all sometimes seems impossible. Each person in the family has needs and desires. But whose needs come first when there is a conflict, as there often is? Impatience and surface living masquerade as the norm.

WORKING THROUGH THE DILEMMA

What can you do if you find yourself in a similar situation? First, as an individual or couple, name the three main objectives you want to accomplish with your life. Let's walk through an example. Your objectives might be (1) to have happy marriage; (2) to raise responsible, well-adjusted children; and (3) to make a meaningful contribution to the world.

Second, list all of your commitments for an average week. HUSBAND: Work, racquetball and workouts, church attendance, upkeep on house and yard, help with chores, attend kids' events. WIFE: Work part-time, housework, laundry, cooking, chauffeuring kids, attend ladies' church group, attend kids' events. Then add all of the extras, either planned or unplanned: errands, volunteer work, lunch out with friends, sports events, shopping, doctors' appointments.

Third, circle the things on your list that have caused you the most frustration. Could you have eliminated them with better planning, more self-discipline to decline invitations, or a change in a nonproductive habit? Then place a square around the items that aren't good or bad, but don't move you toward one of your three life objectives. If you have a long list, you may even need to place a square around those commitments that meet your objectives but cause an overload because there are too many all at one time.

Fourth, do some surgery. Eliminate from your schedule those squared and circled items that are not crucial to reaching your objectives. Maybe the committee meeting helps you to feel as though you are making a contribution to society but causes a distance in your family because it requires you to be gone several nights a week, leaving you with little time or energy for family times. Put the committee on hold for a few years and concentrate on building family memories. Perhaps you are drawn to the mall more often than you like to admit. Try limiting your treks to once a week, and make your trips a highlight instead of just something to do.

Fifth, recognize that it is OK to be still. Your worth does not increase or decrease in proportion to how busy you are. As you take the time to really know yourself, opportunities for solitude will become more special to you and your life will be richer for it.

Sixth, call a family council and explain that the pace of your lives cannot continue. Kids and parents alike are getting worn-out, there is no time for togetherness, the family is not enjoying each other anymore, studies are suffering, eating on the run is taking its toll, and thoughtfulness for each other has evaporated.

Affirm the importance of every family member and his or her role in helping the family to become a well-functioning unit. Then present a snapshot of what you, the parents, would like to see in your family. Explain that in order for this ideal state to come to pass, changes must be made and choices determined. For the next session (perhaps a week later) have each child come prepared to share, in order of importance, what his or her most most meaningful activities are. Support one another in the activities each person chooses, realizing they are the ones most important to him.

For the Martins' son Jim, basketball took preeminence on his list. He was willing to give up working for the builder and some of his nights out with his friends. That would allow for adequate time for homework and proper rest, while bringing his family life back into balance. The emphasis on basketball was a choice that meant even more to him because he had to give up other things in order to pursue his personal best. In the end, Jim found that he played better because he wasn't as fatigued and the stress level at home had dropped considerably.

Susan decided that the commercial auditions were not as important to her as gymnastics. And she never really did like piano. Also, she could cut back her baby-sitting from four times a week to one or two. Besides, she missed doing special things with her mother as a result of both of them being too busy.

Joey came to the conclusion that all the hecticness of his young life was just too much for him. He would rather stay home more and play games with his family anyway. But he does like swimming, and his coach said he is pretty good at it, too.

Brad decided to put in a request to his supervisor for a decease in responsibilities, arguing that efficiency was actually being lowered in his department because management was pushing the workers too hard.

Katie felt that attending the children's sports events was a priority, and she let them know how important they were in her planning. In order to bring her own life under more control, she determined to make fewer trips to the grocery store or mall because she just needed one item. She faced the fact that she usually wasted several hours and many more dollars than she should have spent on needless shopping trips. She put her community involvement on hold until she could justify taking the time from more important concerns. She dropped her art class, but felt she needed the social contact and exercise her aerobics class offered.

On our small peninsula and across the channel there are many large trees. When we get a Midwest storm through the area the wind rages and shoots branches in every direction. The next day as light dawns, we see the yard littered with everything from twigs and sticks to large limbs. Just as the wind is a natural cleanser for trees, a crisis can be a natural cleanser for families and the too-active lives we lead. A time of crisis forces us to slow down and concentrate totally on that which is the most important, our values, and even the very foundation of our lives. How wise it would be if we could benefit from an activity cleanser before the crisis strikes.

Beyond the actual time commitment, kids are pressured in another way. Parents sometimes strive to fulfill their wounded egos though their children. As a result, the kids feel undue pressure to perform and bring home trophies, awards, or honors. Twenty-three million children in America participate in organized sports. Violence between parents and the coaches is on the increase. The message parents are sending their kids is that winning is everything and participating just for fun is not an adequate motivation.

One mother in Texas wanted her daughter to be a cheerleader so much that she arranged for the murder of her competitor's mother, hoping the girl would be distraught and drop out from the competition. What a sick value system we have manufactured and continually promote.

Psychology Today reports that "the psychic life of adolescent girls has undergone a dramatic and detrimental change in the past century, especially in terms of their sense of self-worth." In comparing diaries, the researchers found that girls in the past were interested in intellectual and creative activities, books, the arts, and spirituality, whereas today they are obsessed with boys and how to get their attention. A fixation on beauty, grooming, and body image results in feelings of low self-esteem.[1]

Most of our overactivity is self-induced. It is not only the commitments we make or the activities in which we participate that create a hectic lifestyle, but our daily habits unnecessarily overburden us as well. How much of your life is spent doing the same things over and over? Try to simplify repetitive processes to cut down on busyness. If you routinely iron your clothes in the morning and have to set up the iron and ironing board, do all of your ironing for the week at one time. You will you save accumulative time in the mornings and will economize on energy as well.

Maybe you bring work home from the office along with collecting the day's mail and have a habit of dumping it all on the dining room table or living room couch. Later in the evening you have to gather it all up to take to your home office. Try taking work immediately to your home office upon your arrival. As you think through mundane habits and make appropriate changes, you can eliminate insignificant busyness.

THE TYRANNY OF TELEVISION

Television threatens to consume all but the most vigilant. It causes us to believe, think, act, and buy in ways we would not have otherwise. It is subtle in its power and bold in its assumptions. As an activity, watching television has become one of the most destructive of our modern society.

One writer notes that after "nearly 50 years of daily practice in front of the television, we've developed a society dependent upon instant stimulation. The human mind doesn't grow by feeding on 35 television channels, nor does the human body develop through using a TV remote control. But the human spirit is restless and wants a change . . . quick!"[2]

In *Christian Advocate* magazine, Lou Stopps tells of a father who is very concerned about the affects of television on our children: "I would never let my children ever come close to a TV set these days. It's awful what they're doing." And who is that father? "He's Vladimir Zworkin, age 92, and the man who invented the first television tube back in the 1930's!" Stoops reports.[3]

Television desensitizes us to evil and increases our apathy toward good. It encourages violence, greed, and immorality while discouraging kindness, honesty, and fidelity. It glorifies the wealthy while debasing the poor. And yet, we continue to make excuses for watching television even as the filth filters through our minds. Is it from a lack of creativity in filling those hours with more meaningful interchanges? Is it because we are enticed by depravity and feel helpless in its clutches?

Is it because we are trying to escape having time to think and perhaps face an unattractive trait in ourselves? Is it because it is easier to let the kids watch what they want than to be constantly engaged in battle? Is it because we want to experience life vicariously through false scenarios because our lives seem dull in comparison? Is it because we are lonely and lack the skills to reach out to make new friends? Is it because we are trying to lift a sagging self-esteem by pretending to be knowledgeable of the latest happenings in the electronic prison?

David had this to say about television in our newsletter, *Downscaling 46510:*

> Television. For years we never had one of our own. Not because we couldn't afford it, but because we simply elected not to for a number of reasons. As a result, our girls became prolific readers and excellent students.
>
> Then last year as we were in the process of cutting ties with my career, we chose to homeschool our eighth grader. The program was an excellent video school which necessitated the purchase of a you know what.
>
> The process began. Slowly. First, the winter Olympics; then the summer. Then . . . The box is a thief. It steals the little time we have as husbands and families; time to read, do projects, play games, talk, or just think. We wouldn't knowingly invite a thief into our homes (Would we?).[4]

A book by a former television newsperson and anchor, *All That Glitters* (Moody, 1992), offers an inside look at how television operates and the motivation that fuels many of the decisions made by television executives. It will also give you suggestions of ways you can help your children deal with the lure of television.

It may take some tough discipline to wean yourself away from too much television. Be sure to replace that time with worthwhile endeavors. Cook something from scratch. Linger with a good book. Visit a long-lost friend. Play a game with your youngster. It is beneficial to place several TV-free days on your schedule rather than just limiting the hours per day. A sense of peace pervades the atmosphere on those evenings when the intrusive box is silent.

When you are overwhelmed by living, remove yourself physically from stressful situations, get enough rest, change your attitude, and invest in friendships. Are you addicted to the stimulation activity provides? It may be that that very stimulation is wearing you out. Are you inflating the role of trivia in your life while ignoring the more important concerns? Step back and consider your ways.

When we lived in Alaska the kids bought a pair of female hamsters. It wasn't long before we found out they were not both females. Soon the original hamsters became grandparents and their large cage was becoming crowded. As generation after generation of hamsters multiplied, their living quarters had to be continually adapted. Kathy drew the line one day when she went to take a bath and found that twenty-six fluffy creatures had overtaken the tub. One or two hamsters, or even a few, are cute and make satisfactory pets. But when they become prolific to the point of the ridiculous, they become a nuisance and an irritation. It is the same way with activities. Overcrowding detracts from the specialness of each activity until our schedules reach an absurd state. What about it? Do you and your family need to get rid of some hamsters?

NOTES

1. "Dear Diary," *Psychology Today* 25, no. 3 (May/June 1992), 18.
2. Stephen A. Bly, "Are We Having Fun Yet?" *Moody*, June 1992, 16.
3. Lou Stoops, "Family Moments," *Christian Advocate*, July 1992, 18.
4. David Babbitt, "Just Thoughts," *Downscaling 46510*, October 1992, 2.

15

What's Your Enjoyment IQ?

Shortly after our arrival in Africa, Dave went on an overnight flight to a remote outstation. It was the first night Kathy had spent there with just the children. After they were asleep, she made her way up the hill to visit with the station's hostess. There was a full moon, so she didn't even need a flashlight. Since the area was heavily influenced by mission organizations, Kathy had a false sense of security. On this particular night, the visit extended longer than she had intended. As she made her way over the path and down the stone stairway, the moonlight guided her.

Just after getting into bed, Kathy noticed a dark figure descending those same stairs. A moment later a flashlight shown in the window at the back of the house. Now perplexed, Kathy got up as soon as the flashlight moved to the next window. She followed its path from window to window, fright mounting with each passing second. Then came the rattle of bottles and cans in the storage shed. Whoever it was, was intent on finding something there. Watching from a nearby window Kathy considered her alternatives. If she went out and confronted the thief, he might have a machete and chop her to pieces. If she remained silent, he might get away. So she sneaked out the front door to a neighbor's house and tried to wake them. By the time they were aroused from a deep sleep and went with Kathy back to the shed, the intruder was gone.

The next morning confirmed the theft. The incident terrified Kathy. That night she woke up with a start after dreaming about the dark figure she had seen the night before outside the window. A few nights later, she sat up with a gasp after seeing the figure in her sleep, now at her bedroom door. The next night she dreamed that he was hunched over her sleeping body, ready to pounce. She screamed and screamed. Then she felt his arms grab her and shake her, and she screamed all the louder. When she finally awoke, Dave was holding her and shaking her, trying to wake her up.

Too often we are oblivious to the dangers of our rat-race existence. Like Kathy on that moonlit evening, we go about our way unprepared for potential hazards. We think we are safe because we think the way we are living is the path to success. But just around the corner lurks calamity. If we are not watchful, it will overtake us.

We imagine we must be enjoying life because we are busy scurrying to and fro. Perhaps in our dreams the thing we fear is drawing closer: the fear that life may be meaningless after all, the fear that if we stop too long we will see ourselves up close and be disappointed, the fear that we will have lived in vain. Only by someone shaking us awake will we escape a life overwrought with activity and busyness but devoid of meaning and true enjoyment.

WHAT ABOUT YOU?

Contemplate the following questions and consider if perhaps you are coming too close to danger and are unable to really enjoy life because you are bogged down with feelings of inadequacy, past failures, or future worries. Let the honesty of your answers shake you awake to help you see that much of what you fear is only in your mind and that you can take steps now to live a more enjoyable life.

1. Are you afraid of happiness? Is it out of your comfort zone? Are you threatened by leisure time?
2. What makes you laugh? What makes you cry?
3. Do you have vitality and an intense interest in living? Are you intimate with life or are you afraid of experiencing it to the fullest?
4. Do you enjoy those things that you must do?
5. Do you feel that you are fighting against everybody and everything?

6. Do you regularly take a moment to appreciate the beauty within youself? Your kindness to others, your sense of humor, your organizational ability, your strong mind?
7. Do you feel as though you want to escape life, or do you embrace it?
8. How can you expand your horizons?
9. Is it time to change something about yourself? (Update your looks, change obnoxious or rude behavior, delete sarcasm or negativism from your conversation?)
10. Do you focus too intently on yourself?
11. How do you play games—to win or to help others enjoy the game? There is greater satisfaction in having fun together and not being too concerned about winning.
12. What role does your background and upbringing have on your freedom to express happiness?
13. What do you find pleasure in?
14. Are you spending your energies more on problems or on possibilities?
15. Think about the things that are the most important to you. What if you knew you would lose them in three months? How would your life change between now and then?
16. Do you place too much importance on what others think? Is it keeping you from being freely happy?

17. Are you generally discontent?
18. Do you feel you have given up your chance of being happy today because of some failure in the past?
19. Do you have the freedom to do without, so that you can give to another?
20. When do you feel most bound?
21. Are you denying yourself enjoyment of life until circumstances are just right? We may end up postponing joy our whole lives.
22. What makes someone fun to live with? Are you fun to live with?
23. List ten ways you have grown deeper in the last decade.
24. Is the pain of regret keeping you from moving forward?
25. Are you living the moments of your life halfheartedly?
26. Do you pass your stress on to others, making their lives miserable? Relaxation techniques may not be a permanent solution if you fail to deal with the underlying cause.
27. Do you feel free to give love away? When was the last time you allowed yourself to love unselfishly?
28. Is your anxiety over the future destroying your enjoyment of the present? Is your depression over the past encroaching on your happiness today?
29. Are you feeling sorry for yourself for any reason?
30. Do you view life as a problem to be solved, or an enjoyment to be welcomed?

HINTS FOR A HAPPIER LIFE

Often by putting in a little extra effort, we can receive rich dividends of happiness. If you have found your enjoyment level going stale over the last few years, try a few of these ideas and notice the difference it makes in your life.

1. Give yourself permission to be happy.
2. Be less serious. Try it for a day, then two.
3. Act on a spontaneous impulse to do something fun.
4. Recognize the correlation between an obsession to acquire things and a decrease in happiness.

5. Stop trying to control people. You only push them farther away and keep yourself from enjoying them for who they are.
6. Identify one or two things you want to accomplish each day, and then take the time to celebrate their completion.
7. Feel the texture of everyday happenings, appreciating the small things that make up life.
8. Visit a card shop. Buy someone a humorous card. Read the cards with your spouse and share the funniest with each other.
9. Develop better eye contact and a smile.
10. What's wrong with rose colored glasses once in a while?
11. Exercise and get in shape to have energy for extras and to enjoy more fully what you do.
12. Learn to think like a kid—they naturally know how to have fun; have inquisitive, curious, and flexible minds; and allow themselves to be vulnerable.
13. Try something new—a unique adventure or experience.
14. Spend time with happy people.
15. Set aside a "Be Happy" day. On that day, make a conscious choice to be happy all day. Happiness is a discipline, an art, and a gift to be shared.
16. Give music a greater role in helping you to find pleasure in life.
17. Choose to be thankful; list your problems and be thankful for what you will learn through them.
18. Choose to forgive. None of us can escape being hurt though life.
19. Select one person a day to make a difference in their lives —to encourage, uplift, and inspire. Make life come alive for them.
20. Try vicarious joy. Find someone who is rejoicing in a recent victory, promotion, or new birth in the family. Enjoy their happiness with them.
21. Do something worthwhile today that will have a lasting effect.
22. Lean into life, your pain, and your problems instead of fighting against them. Learn what you can, and become a better person because of it.

23. Determine to laugh at yourself the next time something would be funny if it wasn't happening to you. And the next . . .
24. Fully appreciate one stimulus before advancing to another. Reflect on a kindness someone showed to you, delight in the lightness of a child's laughter, linger over the aroma of a roast in the oven or fresh-made bread.
25. Anticipate high-stress events and focus on something pleasurable that will come about afterward rather than on the event itself. (Stressful event: job interview. Pleasurable aftermath: getting together with a friend after the interview.)
26. Change your perception of a negative situation and invent a creative alternative.
27. Get organized for greater enjoyment and peace.
28. Start the collection or other hobby you always wanted to someday.
29. Do something fun all by yourself. (Ice skate at the mall, explore a new section of town, take a bike ride.)
30. Adopt a kid for a day. Children hug life, not hold it at arm's length.
31. Think of a time when you did something that was meaningful to you. Do it again.
32. Really listen the next time someone talks to you.
33. Buy yourself a flower or a card. To you from you.
34. Put up a bird feeder. In the winter, the birds will keep you entertained.
35. Start an aquarium. It adds interest and movement.
36. Increase your selection of indoor plants for health and restfulness.
37. Get outside more. We are becoming indoor, sedentary creatures.
38. Meet for lunch with a new friend.
39. Be more affectionate (appropriately), especially to family members, through words and hugs.
40. Allow yourself the freedom to do nothing once in a while.

MISCELLANEOUS THOUGHTS

Our appreciation of and capacity for health, warmth, joy, fullness, and friendships will increase in proportion to our experience of sickness, cold, pain, hunger, and loneliness. We need to be careful that our survival and coping mechanisms do not drive us to bitterness but rather allow us to develop character. We have a tendency as human beings to avoid pain, to try to escape it, no matter what the eventual cost.

Missed opportunities are like missed sunsets. If we are lounging and notice the rays of pink on the wall but don't feel like getting up at that moment to enjoy it, when we do finally get up, the sunset is gone along with all its majesty. There will be another, but never the same one again.

Archibald Hart says, "If you want to be full of joy you will need to slow down. You will have to sleep more, play more and spend time with your loved ones. You may have to settle for fewer stimulating and exciting activities and rediscover the elementary pleasure of boredom and the delight of simple things."[1]

Kathy had some notes in her file on a study of 450 people who lived to be one hundred years of age. (Unfortunately she didn't record the source.) The following characteristics were found. They led active lives; used moderation in everything; ate lightly and simply; had fun; were early to bed and early to rise; were free from worry and fear, especially the fear of death; had serene minds with faith in God. Other traits worth cultivating: optimism, leading a meaningful life, having realistic expectations and aspirations, and developing close relationships.

"Children laugh an average of 400 times a day, but adults laugh an average of only 15 times daily," the author of an article in *Glamour* magazine says.[2] To help you trigger those happy feelings, digest a page or two of *14,000 Things to Be Happy About*, by Barbara Ann Kipfer (New York: Workman, 1990). The book, the author says, "represents 20 years of recording all the little things that make me happy."

"Facial feedback" is the theory that since our faces reflect emotion, if we purposely mimic various emotions, we will take on the feeling associated with the facial expression. A look of sadness will produce a feeling of sadness. A look of happiness, anger, or fear will produce those emotions. The theory is based on research showing that using the forty-two facial muscles in a contrived smile produced the same physical reactions in the brain as an authentic smile did.[3] The premise is that if we think first, then act on those thoughts, corresponding emotions will follow, rather than waiting for feelings to direct our actions. Some ways we can put this concept into practice: showing love to a spouse where feelings have dwindled, being excited about life, being grateful for hard times.

William R. Mattox, Jr., reports that "when 1,500 schoolchildren were asked, 'What do you think makes a happy family?' social scientists Nick Stinnett and John DeFrain [discovered] that children did not list money, cars, fine homes or televisions.' Instead the answer most frequently offered was 'doing things together.'"[4] Are you providing a happy home environment for your children?

Traditionally, the family dinner hour set the stage for closeness and happy bantering about the day. Today, however, eating out has become a trend of busier lifestyles, emphasizing convenience. Americans spend more than 40 percent of their food dollar eating out.[5]

We recently met a couple who had two extremes of the family dinner hour as they grew up. The husband recounted:

> We were forced to eat a meal that resembled a full-course Sunday dinner every night. We sometimes had to stay for hours while we politely dined. We all waited until everyone had an opportunity to dish up their food before we began eating. We often resented having to take so much time to eat. The first time I ate at my wife's house was when we were in high school. She has eleven sisters and brothers. Their mealtime was more of a race. I remember waiting politely to begin eating until all the food was passed. Much to my surprise, everyone was finished before I took my first bite!
>
> But now, we have gone too far the other way. We eat on the run. We do require dinner out after church, but there is not a lot of table space in a restaurant for five kids. We try to get a group rate. We either pull two tables together or everyone clamors to be able to eat by himself. But mom usually wins out and gets to sit by herself. (Just kidding.) We have a formal dining room that only gets used twice a year for eating.

How would you describe the effect your mealtime has on the health and happiness of your family? What steps could you take to make a change for the better?

The woman in an earlier chapter who had started a successful cottage industry, then began to feel ruled by that same business, made the decision to abandon the business and the rat race that went with it.

> Last November, on the spur of the moment, I decided to close my business. Everybody had their hands out for my affection and care, but I couldn't see that. I also couldn't see that by this time my husband was making a perfectly good salary we could live on with a little compromise. What I did see was bitterness and a sense of failure as a person. Yes, I was making $1,000 a week, but the cost was ruinous.
>
> Now—I play. I stay home and write fiction and poetry and my column. I have a few part-time jobs that are fun and produce only vacation money that I put in a special account all year. As a professor, my husband gets three months off in the summer. With what I saved since November, we can all play all summer. Time is the only perk a professor has—that and free textbooks and a pocket full of chalk. I can't tell you how nice it is to cut down and relax and be able to say, "No, we can't afford it." Actually neither us has any desire for things—just time.[6]

VACATION ALTERNATIVES

"According to a Louis Harris poll, the amount of leisure time available to the average American has shrunk from about 26 to 17 hours per week."[7] So says the author of an article in a magazine on health. With so little leisure time, vacations may be needed more than ever. Not only do they give a break in routine, they can be the springboard for creating family memories and togetherness. Family-style vacations are having an impact on the travel industry. Hotels are catering to families with children, complete with baby-proof rooms and supervised activity centers. Camping has seen a resurgence in interest as the hustle and bustle of everyday life leaves no time for walks in the woods or getting away from noise pollution.

Careful planning will enhance your vacation. If you sign with a package deal, make sure you read the fine print to avoid disappointment later. For a free brochure and guide to National Parks send a self-addressed, stamped business envelope to: Discover America's Parks with Mott's, c/o 1500 Broadway, 25th Floor, New York, NY

10036. There are organizations that provide a vacation along with tax deductions if you volunteer to help the organization in the process. Send $5.00 to American Hiking Society, 1015 31st Street, N.W., Washington, D.C. 20007; (202) 385-3252), for a list of volunteer jobs on public lands.

Coming of age is the idea of swapping homes for vacations. Intervac (800-756-HOME) charges $45.00 to list your home and receive their catalog of 8,000 properties for exchange. Vacation Exchange Club, established in 1960, has 16,000 members in 50 countries. You stay in another member's home, either in the United States or overseas, and they stay in yours. Arrange your stay for a few days to a few months and pay no hotel bills. By taking advantage of an exchange program, your vacation dollars can be spent on costs other than lodging. The annual membership fee of $50.00 provides you with a listing in and a copy of their directory. There are no other fees. You make all the arrangements with another family. For more information write: Vacation Exchange Club, P.O. Box 650, Key West, FL 33041; (800) 638-3841.

Servas (meaning serve) is a cooperative system of hosts and travelers promoting peace and understanding between nationalities. You plan the trip along with a list of hosts in the country you wish to visit (usually for two-day stays). Or you can become a host to provide simple accommodations and perhaps meals. Servas requests a contribution of $45.00 per year per traveler to cover Servas expenses. Stays with the hosts are free. Write: U.S. Servas, Inc., 11 John Street, Rm. 407, New York, NY 10038; (212) 267-0252.

If you would like more information on vacation exchanges, bed and breakfast exchanges, or hospitality exchanges, *The Vacation Home Exchange and Hospitality Guide,* by John Kimbrough, is available for $16.95, including shipping. Order from: Kimco Communications, 4242 W. Dayton, Fresno, CA 93722; (209) 275-0893.

Rolling Ventures is a newsletter encouraging earning an income while traveling in your RV. Subscriptions (four issues per year) are $18.00. Write: *Rolling Ventures,* #1404, P.O. Box 2190, Henderson, NV 89009-2109; (800) 437-2431.

Organized family camping programs are another alternative. "According to *USA Today,* the cost of a vacation in the U.S. in 1991 averaged $159.70 per day for a family of four. According to a recent Christian Camping International/USA survey, the cost for a family of four to attend a CCI camp or conference center was about $84.50 per day."[8] (You can contact Christian Camping International by phoning 800-767-1675.)

When we were going full-steam into researching and writing this book we were faced with implementing the principle of relationships first. Here's how Dave described it in his publisher's letter for our monthly newsletter:

> Indian summer was full upon us. As I stood basking in its glory, the aroma of burning leaves, warm air on my face, leaves rustling about my feet against a background of brilliantly colored trees, and the taste of warm cider all combined to open my treasure chest of memories packed away many years ago. It had been nearly twenty years since they had been reviewed, yet there they were, as unfaded as when they were first made.
>
> After interrupting my reverie, we packed up our bikes and headed for one of the most beautiful bicycle trails I've ever ridden. We rode and talked, picnicked and enjoyed this glorious Indian summer; packing as many memories into my daughter's treasure chest as we could for her to review at some later date. I'm glad I had, and took the time, to make those memories. We can either make Indian summer memories or harsh, cold, drab winter memories for our kids. I've made too many of the latter.[9]

What kind of memories are you building and enjoying these days?

NOTES

1. Archibald D. Hart, *Unlocking the Mystery of Your Emotions* (Waco, Tex.: Word, 1979, 1989), 144.

2. Stephanie Young, "Laugh, It's Healthy," *Glamour,* December 1992, 33.

3. Judith Stone, "What's in Her Smile?" *American Health* 9, no. 7 (September 1990), 32–33.

4. William R. Mattox, Jr., "The Parent Trap, So Many Bills, So Little Time," *Policy Review,* Winter 1991, 13.

5. "Eating Out Is Result of Busier Lifestyles," *The Paper,* 9 September 1991.

6. "Letter of the Month," *Downscaling 46510,* June 1992, 3.

7. In *Health* (May/June 1991), 43.

8. Interview with Bob Kobielush, "Christian Camps," Christian Camping International advertising (1992).

9. David Babbitt, "Just Thoughts," *Downscaling 46510,* November 1992, 2.

Attitudes for Sale

PART 6

16

Caution:
The Greener Grass
May Contain Pesticides

lexis De Tocqueville said of Americans, "It is odd to watch with
what feverish ardor [they] pursue prosperity. Ever tormented
by the shadowy suspicion that they may not have chosen the
shortest route to get it, they cleave to the things of this world
as if assured that they will never die, and yet rush to snatch any that
comes within their reach as if they expected to stop living before
they had relished them. Death steps in, in the end, and stops them
before they have grown tired of this futile pursuit of that complete
felicity which always escapes them."[1]

Recently we watched with interest a special educational program on the Donner Party of 1846. We had looked for real estate
and considered settling in the same location as the subject of the
documentary. It was a story of prosperous families from the Midwest looking for the greener grass of California. Eighty-seven travelers started out on the 2,500-mile journey over plains, mountains,
rivers, and deserts. Horror after horror awaited them on the trail.
In the end only forty-six survived the gruesome trip. Cannibalism
and insanity were to infiltrate the camp before the party was finally
rescued in the Sierra Nevada Mountains near Lake Tahoe. That
fateful location is now called Donner Pass.[2]

Instead of greener grass, what the Donner Party found was a
tale of suffering we can hardly even imagine. What about us? To
what lengths will we go in our search for the "good life" when all
along we probably already possess it? Whether it be for beauty,

friendship, a higher standard of living, or greater job satisfaction, a change in attitude may be all that's necessary to appreciate what we have instead of lamenting what we don't. "Some women try every new beauty product. Some diet daily. Others exercise endlessly. And still they're not happy. . . . Preoccupation with looks occurs because society has made appearance too significant," the author of an article in *USA Today* observes.[3]

The technology that has increased the number of products available to us has also enabled us to learn of those products. Advertisers create and fuel mass insecurity to the point of continual discontent with what we have. "About 100 years ago a survey asked average Americans to list their wants—they listed 70. In a similar survey, Americans recently listed 500."[4] Why not answer that question yourself?

Perhaps it is because we have had tremendous opportunities over the life of our marriage, but when Kathy answered that same question, she came up with only five "wants," and most of those dealt with intangibles. Or maybe it's because we have found that "things" don't really satisfy, and seeking after them is useless in terms of living a meaningful life.

The authors of an article in *U.S. News and World Report* note that "even in the best of times, the American family seems to be fraying. But these are not the best of times."[5] How much of the demise of the American family could be attributed to parents searching for that greener grass while ignoring the care of their own. They won't allow themselves to be content until everything matches the unrealistic world of television, so they keep striving for that end. But they strive in vain, for none of life matches a staged illusion. In their search, many discover, too late, that they were living on the greener grass all along.

RELEASING EXPECTATIONS
AND OTHER NEGATIVE ATTITUDES

Much of our frustration and dissatisfaction with our lot in life originates from the importance we place on our expectations. The greater the expectation, the greater the disappointment if it isn't filled. By releasing our expectations, we can stop comparing, measuring, and worrying. In doing so, we will more enjoy any process

we undertake. We live in an imperfect world. We are imperfect people. The ideal does not exist anywhere except in God Himself. If you tend toward perfectionism, are your standards based on unresolved guilt, self-justification, anxiety, or defensiveness? By demanding perfection of ourselves, others, or circumstances, we will be bound by discontent, shallowness, and defeat.

While working on this book we set goals for its completion. In order to finish by the deadline, we needed to research, interview, compile and organize the material, and then do the actual writing and initial editing. As it turned out, the research took longer than either of us could have imagined. For the most part we took it in stride, although as the months to the deadline became weeks, frustration was mounting. One chapter in particular took several weeks longer than we had expected. Because our expectations were not being met, we felt frustration all the more keenly. We needed to declare a halt to our expectation level and continue to do the best we could. It relieved some internal pressure to remind ourselves that we had been giving the project our all for months and then to throw out what proved to be unrealistic expectations.

Although we believe this project warrants our best effort, not everything we do justifies the time and effort necessary to give our best. We all have limitations. Limitations are not necessarily negative. They help us define, clarify, and accept our boundaries. It is imperative that each of us selects those projects, plans, and people in which he will invest his best. We may need to do away with certain activities, endeavors, or friendships that will then enable us to have the energy and time needed to invest in the most worthwhile. Then there are those things we must do, but do not require our top-of-the-line input. Time management experts agree that it is best to plan to use your high energy and mentally alert times for those periods that require your best. Other routine tasks can be adequately covered in our lower energy, duller thinking intervals. Examine your priorities, eliminate the unnecessary, and elevate the important.

Longing for greener grass is keenly felt in the area of personal considerations. We spend hundreds of dollars every year on our outer appearance. Many have the mistaken notion that our worth is determined by our clothes and appearance. The more we invest in that appearance, the thinking goes, the more will be our personal worth. Yet an inordinate fixation on self destroys any chance for meaningful interchange with others. How often have you met someone who was beautiful on the outside but so wrapped up in himself that his shallowness left you gagging?

By looking nice without an overpreoccupation with self, we achieve a healthy balance. Rather than focusing on impressing others, when we know we are presenting our best we can have an inner confidence that will free us to concentrate on others. Our attitudes and countenance should clothe us with grace as well, but how often we ignore their impact on others. Not only do we more favorably impress others and like ourselves better when we are pleasant, but it is also good for our health. One author notes: "People who are slow to anger, optimistically look for the good in others and treat everybody with consideration have stronger immune systems and fewer heart attacks than hostile, cynical people."[6] Hostility can be just as dangerous health-wise as high cholesterol or smoking.

If you met someone who looked and acted exactly like you, what would your impression be? Would you like you and want to be around you? Try this exercise. Monitor and record people's responses when you smile, show kindness, listen intently, exhibit patience and humility, exude confidence, pass on compliments, speak with a musical voice, express delight, portray enthusiasm and energy, and show generosity. Compare those reactions to the ones you get when you are negative, scowling, arrogant, rude, apathetic, self-ish, or impatient. How do you feel about yourself in the two types of situations? Maybe the dissatisfaction we feel regarding our circumstances is not because of the circumstances themselves, but because of our outlook toward them. Changing locales, jobs, partners, or families will not alter our satisfaction levels, because we carry our dissatisfaction within ourselves.

What about our speech? Do we think our grass will be greener if we adopt the patterns of the successful and intelligent? Complex speech style may give us an air of importance, but does it communicate? One day when Kathy picked up Dave at the airport, he had a newsmagazine with him. On the way home Kathy read the cover story with rapt interest—not because of the subject, but because she was drooling with awe over the author's command of vocabulary, projection of intelligence through his writing, and learned style. Her writing in comparison was straightforward, simplistic, and readable. When she said as much to Dave, he replied, "The reason I bought the magazine was for the cover article. But I read a few paragraphs and the guy didn't make sense. He wasn't communicating." (And Dave has had nine years of university level education.) Not that Kathy could understand the author any better, but he sure sounded intelligent.

It was then that she gave up the notion (expectation) that her writing would have more value if it sounded complicated and academic. Kathy is the kind of person who identifies with Anne of Green Gables, who loved to use words people just shook their heads over. Intricate and perplexing phrases feel good rolling off her tongue. She's gotten used to taming the urge to speak in flowery syllables that no one understands. Daughter Kimberly says Kathy likes to make things complicated just so she has something to think about. Problem is, not everyone wants to spend his free time thinking, so she had better communicate simply and clearly. (Dave also chides Kathy for the number of words she makes up just because they sound as though they *should* be words.) We heard it said once that the more deeply you think, the more important it is for you to communicate simply.

Most of us run toward the mirage of green grass at one time or another. Gayle left the Midwest looking for excitement because her career needed a boost and because she wanted to get away from her hometown. She liked telling her relatives and old friends that she had a sales job in Texas. But after a few years she began to miss the intangibles those same relatives and friends offered. She had already made the decision to return when she received a large bonus check. Her sales manager asked if she would stay if she got a million dollar account and received more of those bonus checks. Gayle told him it wouldn't matter, because she wasn't happy in what she was doing and missed her family and friends. The money wasn't worth it. By being content in who you are and learning to enjoy what is and not only what could be, you will soon see the grass in the distance fade while your own takes on new life.

When Jeannette was twenty she said, "I'm not ready to meet the person I'm going to marry because *I'm* not the person I hope to be when I get married." That's a profound concept. We are all changing and becoming. Denying the myth of the greener grass does not negate the necessity of growth. From time to time we need object lessons to help us make appropriate changes—an important letter ruined because we forgot to check the pockets before we tossed them into the machine; a damaged friendship because of our insensitivity; an empty checking account because of our indulgence; or embarrassment because of our disorganization.

Much of what we do that could be keeping us chained to an unsatisfying life may not be borne of conscious thought. It may be only the result of early conditioning. When Kathy was growing up, she and her three sisters had many outdoor toys and bikes. There was always a scurry when an afternoon thunderstorm suddenly appeared on the horizon. "Quick! Put the bikes on the porch, get the toys into the playhouse, take down the blanket tent from the swing frame, pick up all the supplies from playing school, and do a once-over on the yard to make sure we've got everything!" That same tendency stayed with her for years every time there was an afternoon storm, but she came up empty in retrieving things that could get damaged in the rain. So why did she always feel as though she had to do a "once-over" in the yard? It was childhood conditioning that was necessary at the time, but no longer served its purpose in adulthood. Are there ingrained attitudes or practices in your life that serve no purpose and could easily be changed to make contentment a reality for you?

When you make a significant change in your life, keep in mind that you may decide it is easier to accept minor discomfort over a long period of time than intense discomfort for a shorter period of time. That is because the tendency is to give up if things get worse before they get better. (And they usually do because that is the nature of change.) Change requires accepting responsibility for our actions, perseverance, and the courage to go forward despite distressing setbacks.

Change is always easier when you have a support system. The University of Michigan Institute on Social Research found that of 37,000 participants, those who had little support from family and friends had twice as many serious illnesses and a higher death rate five to twelve years later.[7] Support systems offer mutual encouragement, care, concern, inspiration, and the benefit of learning from another's failures.

Look around you. What can you be grateful for right now? Do you have a warm place to sleep? A family? A job? Food? Friends? An interesting hobby? Dissatisfaction feeds the illusion of the greener grass syndrome. We are willing to believe the illusion because sometimes it is easier to fantasize than to face reality. The pesticides we apply in that search for the illusive greener grass leave a bitter taste. Betrayal and anger set in. Betrayal by a society that promises fulfillment through wealth or prestige. Anger at ourselves for believing the myth and allowing it to ruin relationships, ravage health, and corrupt contentment. Add a little T.L.C. to your own grass and watch it take on a deeper green by the month.

NOTES

1. Alexis De Tocqueville, as quoted on "The American Experience" 28 October 1992, by WGBH Educational Foundation, WNET.

2. Ibid.

3. Nancy Hellmich, "Finding a Fix for Society's Body Fixation," *USA Today*, 12 June 1992, 2D.

4. Kathy Collard Miller, "How *Content* Are You?" *Today's Christian Woman* 14, no. 1 (January/February 1992), 41.

5. Don. L. Boroughs with David Hage, Robert F. Black, and Richard J. Newman, "Love and Money," *U.S. News and World Report*, 19 October 1992, 54.

6. Catherine Houck, "How to Prevent Disease Without Dieting, Exercise or Drugs," *Woman's Day*, 24 September 1991, 40.

7. Ibid., 38.

17

Service with a Smile

Y ou see them everywhere. You yank a curtain over the corner of your mind that threatens to implicate your heart. You try—but you are unsuccessful, and for a moment you feel their pain, you hear their cries of anguish, you see their wretched bodies malformed from hunger. Then you walk away, or turn the page, or flip the channel. The moment has passed, and you are safe. Safe from feeling their torment deeply enough to help alleviate their misery. The poor. The suffering. Who are they? Why does their plight gnaw at the pit of our stomachs?

The writer of an article in *Woman's Day* says, "They come every day, these tragedies and terrors, into the peace and chaos of my kitchen, and every day I hesitate before I throw them in the trash. If I look at them it breaks my heart, and just now I can't afford to have my heart broken. We are in a recession; I am losing my job; I am a single mother with children to raise. So I harden myself against opening them at all. Then I watch my healthy children playing, I take the cookies out to cool, and deep inside I know that—just as the letter writers say—I could choose to help instead."[1]

In your own way are you doing anything to help alleviate the suffering in the world? Maybe your efforts won't make front page news. Maybe what you do won't win any medals. Perhaps your small financial investment won't save all the starving children. But if you helped save just one life, or encouraged just one young mother in the grip of depression, or showed love to a neglected child, or made just one homeless person's plight a little easier to bear, then you have made a difference. And the surprising thing is—you may well have found happiness in the process.

Carla Rohlfing, in an article titled "Why You're Feeling Stressed," says that "mental health experts are becoming increasingly aware that feeling time pressured is just one of many factors that has led to a new stressor that is overwhelming Americans: emotional isolation. . . . Experts also point to another more surprising source of the isolation epidemic: The until-now ballyhooed emphasis on the self in American society."[2] The futility of selfishness in the '80s gave birth to the fruitfulness of benevolence in the '90s. *The Washington Post* reports that historian Arthur Schlesinger, Jr., believes that "Americans are at the end of a 30-year cycle of self-absorption" and that there are "signs that generosity may be coming back in style."[3] *The Wall Street Journal* notes that "almost 40 million Americans take the time to care. . . . Better-educated and working people are more likely to volunteer than others. Nearly 40% of those with four or more years of college volunteer time, compared with 8% of high school dropouts."[4]

It is not only adults that are giving of themselves to leave their world a better place. One report describes the attitude many young people today demonstrate. "The youth of the '90's are concerned about their world. With creativity and ingenuity, they're taking positive steps toward correcting problems facing their communities and making their own futures look brighter. Millions of today's kids are using their energy to solve problems in their own hometowns and create a better place for themselves and future generations. Too often their responsible actions and deeds are overshadowed by today's negative headlines."[5] Mandatory community service is now a requirement in some high schools. The aim is to teach "youth something about selflessness and responsibility."[6]

Volunteer efforts may encompass going beyond our comfort zones to travel to another part of the world. "Thousands of American health care workers . . . leave their commitments at home and rush to Kurdistan, or Bangladesh. . . . Stymied by traditional relief agencies that do not have many assignments overseas for physician volunteers, Americans are turning to the new U.S. affiliates of (foreign agencies)."[7]

One family with eight children still at home decided to bring the world of need and opportunity to a personal level. They went to Ecuador to volunteer for three months, where even the children are involved in helping. Because they live a downscaled lifestyle in the States, they have the funds to undertake a unique service project such as this. Those children will long remember the fulfilling times of serving others. Someone has said, "We tire of those pleasures we take, but never of those we give." How true that is.

In giving to others we may actually be helping ourselves. In *Give to Live,* Douglas M. Lawson reports that "recent studies by *Psychology Today, American Health,* and The Institute for Advancement of Health have referred to a 'helper's high.' Social scientists and doctors are beginning to see how the human mind triggers special chemicals that enable us to feel more expansive, even euphoric. These chemicals, called endorphins, are released during esteem-building activities such as working to help others. The noted Harvard cardiologist and author Dr. Herbert Benson says that altruistic acts can produce a relaxation response equivalent to a deep state of rest."[8]

Lawson also notes that "a ten-year study of the physical health and social activities of 2,700 men in Tecumseh, Michigan, found that those who did regular volunteer work had death rates two and one-half times lower than those who didn't. Those who serve others may be on a new path to longevity."[9] Volunteers receive more enjoyment out of life for they dynamically connect with the pulse of human emotions. It gives them more vitality, enthusiasm, and a deeper ability to deal with their own stress.

Some friends of ours have sacrificed so that others may receive. They consistently avoid excess so that they can save the air fare to go to China to take Bibles where a people hunger for more than food. It is an exhilarating experience for them. "When you look into the eyes of the people, you see a sadness that breaks your heart." Eager hands reach for the Scriptures in their own language. Through translators, the couple communicates with the Chinese and are assured that they could have brought no finer gift. China has changed this couple's lives, and their children are saving to go with the youth group next year. Denying wants here in the States was not always easy, but the reward far outweighed any temporary loss they may have felt.

The authors of *Country Bound!*™ report:

Community is back. Civic pride, social consciousness, grassroots activism: these are the lifeblood of towns, large and small. This widespread yearning for community is showing up in our popular culture. It's why nostalgic movies and TV programs about small towns have become a national pastime. . . . Consider participation in area government. With only 25 percent of the population, rural areas have 75 percent of the local government units in the United States. This enhanced opportunity for citizen involvement also implies an increased role for community leadership. Make your voice heard in local politics.[10]

Personal involvement, rather than just making a contribution, gives a volunteer a crucial sense of being needed. Most volunteers respond to pleas for help rather than seeking out avenues of assistance. Lawson notes: "While millions of people give billions of hours in volunteer activities, only 21% of us seek out the activity or assignment on our own. We are more apt to be reactive than active."[11]

Volunteering has the potential for a great sense of personal accomplishment as well as benefiting others. Wanda Whitsitt, founder of the volunteer Lifeline Pilots, was elected to the Illinois Aviation Hall of Fame for her leadership role in providing free air service to those in distress. When her children were almost grown, she took her first flying lessons. After her proficiency increased, she formed an organization of volunteer pilots to transport patients or other distress cases from one place to another. Lifeline Pilots has become a critical service in the Midwest.[12]

Often it isn't until tragedy strikes that the world notices the selfless giving of an individual. Dennis Byrd of the Jets was partially paralyzed in a football game. Angela, Dennis's wife, sent this message to the waiting avalanche of press shortly after the injury: "Tell them Dennis says he's glad God chose him for this, because he has the strength to handle it. And tell them I'm glad God chose me as Dennis's partner." Dennis Byrd lives a life of constant sacrifice for others in giving his time, energies, and compassion for those less fortunate or hurting.[13] "Love rules without a sword, love binds without a cord" (Anonymous).

Volunteering isn't the only means of serving others. Taking pride and exhibiting joy in your work offers daily opportunities for encouragement. Years ago we crossed paths with a trash man who collected garbage on a city truck. Every week he came by the front of our house, singing and whistling as he threw smelly garbage into the truck. He seemed to love his work and elevated the role of garbage collector to new heights. We thought then that if he could be happy in that job, we had a lesson to learn about happiness.

Or there was the bus driver in downtown Chicago. Last year when we went to Chicago for a conference, a shuttle bus was provided to take us from one location to another. One driver's name was Ellen, and we wished in that brief encounter we had had the presence of mind to get her full name and address. We have never seen such a display of outright joy of living and of someone's making it a personal mission to bring happiness to everyone she met. It was a sight to behold, and it did your heart good to have a brush with her happiness for a moment in time.

By reaching out we enable others to reach in and bless our lives in return. Rearrange your life to accommodate service, whether in your work or out. Be alert to needs and be quick to respond to opportunities that fit within your predetermined life priorities. Develop a servant's heart so that when you are treated like a servant, you will respond graciously and lovingly. Serving others and giving of ourselves "multiplies our joys and divides our sorrows." Give it a try, and soon you will be serving with a smile that is genuine and warm.

NOTES

1. Kathleen Cushman, "Charity Begins at Home," *Woman's Day*, 15 October 1991, 170.

2. Carla Rohlfing, "Why You're Feeling Stressed," *Family Circle*, 22 September 1992, 81.

3. Laura Sessions Stepp, "Focus on Self Has Changed Language of Sacrifice; Charitable Groups Report Attitude of Giving to Feel Good, Not Giving Until It Hurts," *The Washington Post*, 24 March 1991, A21.

4. "One in Five Americans Volunteers Some Time," *The Wall Street Journal*, 31 May 1990, B1.

5. Michele Macchia, "American Kids Truly Care," *The Paper*, 12 August 1992, 8.

6. Stepp, A21.

7. Robin Herman, "Doctors Who Respond to Suffering Abroad," *The Washington Post*, 25 June 1991, 8.

8. Douglas M. Lawson, *Give to Live: How Giving Can Change Your Life* (La Jolla, Calif.: ALTI Publishing, 1991), 15–16.

9. Ibid., 20.

10. Marilyn Ross and Tom Ross, *Country Bound!*™ *Trade Your Business Suit Blues for Blue Jean Dreams* (Buena Vista, Colo.: Communication Creativity, 1992), 344– 45. All quotes from this source are used by permission.

11. Lawson, 15.

12. Janice Rosenberg, "Women Who Make a Difference: Lifeline Pilots," *Family Circle*, 2 June 1992, 15–20.

13. Peter King, "'He Has the Strength,'" *Sports Illustrated*, 14 December 1992, 23.

18

Discovering the Pot of Real Gold

One of Dave's duty stations in the navy enabled us to live on the Chesapeake Bay. Shortly after our arrival, our landlord took us water skiing. Kathy was just learning to ski, and after taking a turn around the bay, she collided with the water. Immediately she began to feel a stinging sensation. When she realized that she had fallen into a mass of huge jellyfish with poisonous tentacles, she began screaming and flailing her arms, trying to get the jellyfish away. This only heightened the piercing stinging of the jellyfish as their tentacles broke apart, causing even more poison to be released. It felt like an age before the boat returned to rescue her. Back on shore the damage was clearly evident. Her body was a red welt from forehead to toes. The local custom was to stand in the shower and pour meat tenderizer all over the welts to pull out the poison and neutralize the allergic reaction.

Maybe something has gotten its tentacles around you, and the harder you flail, the more you become entangled. Perhaps you are being poisoned by past pain and disappointment. In order for that hurt to heal, you will need the tenderizer of forgiveness—for yourself and for others. What is keeping you from forgiving? Is it the desire for revenge, holding on to bitterness, fear of being hurt again, determining he or she doesn't deserve to be forgiven, feeling comfortable in your self-pity, anger at the infringer, or not wanting to let go of your pride? Forgive and loose yourself from the tentacles of unforgiveness and begin to enjoy life anew.

It's been five years now since the death of Martha and Bob's son, Chad. The couple had always made their family a priority. Over the years they made special efforts to attend their children's sports events or other activities. Martha and Bob had felt a real need to develop a closeness with their son and daughter as they were growing up. Many times Bob could have stayed late at work, but he made the conscious choice to be with his family instead.

Chad and his older sister by four years, Marilyn, were very active. Bob thinks Chad's life was so full because it was destined to be so short. In fact, just before his death, Chad had gone with a youth organization to Sweden. Bob and Martha still don't know exactly what happened—Chad was by himself when his car ran under a flatbed trailer and he was killed.

Marilyn and Chad had always been good friends. Bob says he doesn't remember them ever saying cross words to each other. Chad was mature for his age, so it was almost as though Marilyn had the big brother that most girls dream of. They were best friends as well as brother and sister. That's why it was so hard for Marilyn when Chad died. Looking back, Bob is very thankful that he put his family first time and again when it would have been financially advantageous to invest those hours in work. He has happy, warm memories of the years their son was with them. And that's something money can't buy. Should your children's lives be cut short, will you look back knowing you have invested your life in making memories instead of regrets?

In an article in *Entrepreneur*, Stephanie Barlow raises the question of relative success: "During the '80's, pursuing the American dream seemed to require putting in 14-hour days, wearing designer suits and making $150,000 a year. So what if people were too exhausted to enjoy their multimillion-dollar homes, too busy to see their spouses or children, and too stressed to get through their 30's without wandering into heart attack territory. They were successful. Or were they?"[1]

One subscriber of our newsletter sent us a copy of a letter to the editor printed in January 1983 and reprinted here by permission.

The Price of Monetary Success Is Too High: I retired from a company [in] Ohio after 47 years [of] service. Through hard work and long hours I moved up the ladder to president. I sent four children through college and gave my wife everything.

My children are grown and gone, my loving wife has passed away. Tonight as I sit alone bringing in the new year, I realize I paid a big price for big money. My job became my life, interest and hobby. I missed playing games with my kids, camping and fishing. I missed spending time with my loved ones. I missed developing hobbies and outside interest[s] for myself.

Please young people, don't make the same mistake. Yes, take your work serious, work hard. But do not take away a moment from your family that belongs to your family or yourself. Sure my family had every-thing, everything except time together which cannot be replaced with money. I hardly know my children, after all it was mom's job to raise the kids, right? Dead wrong!

Worst of all, with my job being of such overall interest to me, I hardly know myself without it. Please people don't make the same mis-take this old fool has. No matter what anyone says . . . no job is worth the price I have paid . . . no job! By the way . . . the company is doing fine without me. So did my family.

Perhaps, just perhaps, Americans are finally beginning to take this man's message to heart. Stephanie Barlow cites evidence that they have:

By all current indications, status symbols like expensive cars and designer clothing have taken a back seat to concerns about health, the environment and family life. Though financial security is still important, most Americans say they'd like to take a more balanced approach to life —more family, more leisure, more community involvement and less work.

A 1991 survey by Hilton Hotel Corp. illustrates this new American life ethic. Given a list of eight goals, 77 percent of the more than 1,000 adults surveyed listed spending more time with family and friends as their top priority. . . . Spending money on material possessions came in last.[2]

The following is the conclusion to the story of the loan officer we wrote about in an earlier chapter:

One day I just got fed up with the whole thing. I decided it was time to spend time with my family. After all, that's why I have a wife and three kids. We are only on this earth for a short period of time. Why not slow down and enjoy it. I told my boss I wanted to resign from branch manager and go back to being a loan officer. I immediately felt like a burden had been lifted from my shoulders. No more solving everyone else's problems. No more driving a lengthy commute. Within one week my shoulder and chest pain left, not to return. My ulcer has not given me any problems and I have a lot more time for my wife and kids.

My income dropped more than 75% overnight. The next 24 months were rough financially, but we downscaled enough that we made it. I only wish that I had seen it earlier. It was hard to climb that ladder to the top, but it was much harder to downscale that ladder. It's nice not to have to sit down every month and write out 20 some checks. Life is much simpler. I intend to keep it that way.[3]

Whatever your situation, you can begin now to improve your family relationships. Dave was gone frequently during Jeannette's high school years, which she regretted and, although not voiced outwardly, probably resented. With Jeannette going through the teenage years mingled with Dave's frustration at his unavoidable absence, instead of smooth sailing when he was home, there was often conflict. Since Jeannette graduated at sixteen and then spent her summers doing volunteer work away from home, Dave had even less time with her.

Jeannette is now twenty-one and living at home, helping in the family business. She recently spent several weeks in the Washington, D.C. area with a family where she had been a live-in nanny. During that time Dave received the following letter from her. We share it here with her permission to underscore the fact that it is never too late to begin where you are. You can't change the past, but you *can* do something about today . . . and tomorrow . . . and . . .

Dear Dad, I was just sitting here thinking about how wonderful you are—so decided to write and tell you how much I appreciate everything you've done for me since I've been home—like building my house so that I have a perfect place to stay, and helping so much with Kenya [a Lhasa apso puppy she rescued]. I love living at home and really do realize how fortunate I am to have such a great place to live.

I think you're the most sensitive, kind, and considerate man I know or ever will know, even though I complain about how you don't always understand me. And I really value your opinion about the things I should do—that's why I ask you so much. I guess I think that if you think it's a good idea, it must be, because you're so wise. I know we don't tell you often enough how amazing we think you are—you can do just about everything well.

In fact, there's not really anything I don't think my dad can't do. All the building you've done at the house, the business, and your car [a 1974 MG-GBT—he overhauled the engine]—not to mention trying to keep your spoiled girls happy! Anyway, I just wanted to write and tell you how wonderful I think you are, but most of all how lucky I am to have a dad like you. I love you and miss you! I'll be home soon!

Love, Jeannette

P.S. Say hi to Mom and thanks to Kim for taking care of Kenya. I know she's a pain!

We can look back at our lives as parents and isolate those instances when we know we have failed. Although we have made many mistakes over the years, we have confidence that we did our best with who we were and the maturity and knowledge gained to that point. Sure we made mistakes; yes we made unwise decisions. If we could do it over again, with what we know now, we probably would make better choices. But we can't do it over again, and we didn't know then what we do now, so all we can do is go on from here, forgetting what is behind and pressing on toward the future.

If you still have children at home, what are you doing to build mature adults? One report had this to say: "Youth today aren't developing the values they'll need as adults, according to surveys conducted by the Josephson Institute of Ethics and The Search Institute. Both surveys found an unprecedented percentage of American youth cannot tell right from wrong."[4] We have substituted entertainment for chores, amusements for building responsibility, and selfishness for gratitude.

In the search for excellence and in the pressure we place on our kids to perform, perhaps our labor is in vain. As parents we may often wonder if we are doing enough to encourage our kids to excel. Will our allowing them to mature at their own rate, or handing them the responsibility to progress scholastically, or not pushing them harder to continually exceed their personal best in athletics enable them to "make it" as adults? These thoughts bothered Kathy until some years ago. We had encouraged and cheered for our children in academics and athletics, but put the responsibility for their success or failure on them, not on us through applied pressure. But Kathy wondered if we had applied more pressure, would they have reached even greater heights? They were all excellent students, but not the top. They all did well in sports at one time or another and have their share of trophies and ribbons, but their motivation fell short of taking them to the Olympics (although we believe one had the ability—but it wasn't important to her).

One day Kathy learned of a study that concluded that the happiest people are average. Those who are high achievers seem never to be content in what they accomplish—they are always striving for greater heights so happiness eludes them in the present. Those who are underachievers lack the discipline and motivation to accomplish much of anything, hence they lack appreciation of their untapped talents and skills. They are unhappy in their stagnation, but can't seem to muster the "umph" to do anything about it. Those that are "just average" have more balance in their lives and find the enjoyment that seems to bypass the other two groups. The results of that study encouraged Kathy for herself as well. She let up some of her personal pressure to achieve and learned to be more content in just living.

There is pressure all around us. One woman wrote:

> We are surrounded by Amish families who enjoy simplistic lives and rich relationships and I admire that in them. Although I still want my car and electricity, I am looking for ways to simplify my life and my family's lives. My husband is a [name of his profession], so the vast majority of his colleagues are the typical affluent, materialistic breed. We have always lived a moderate lifestyle in comparison to most in our same income bracket, but I am especially interested in "downscaling" even further.

> We are the parents of three kids (under 8) and have been chastised by friends and family for not having all three of them singed up for every conceivable activity. Thank you for giving me a shot of confidence that we are doing what is really pro-family after all. . . . I'm glad to hear that our society is finally re-examining what should come first.[5]

In his search to be the best, one well-known football player compromised his integrity and took steroids to give him the edge over his competition. He believed the onset of his brain cancer was due to the use of steroids over a long period of time. Before his death, he concluded, "There is a lot more to life than just winning!"

From time to time we go to an auction and see a home that is laid out on the lawn or in the barn piece by piece. Old dishes and linens; toys and games; knickknacks and paintings; tools and hardware; furniture and appliances; photos and magazines. It always leaves us with a sad and empty feeling. Here is someone's life reduced to a pile of junk at an estate sale with strangers picking over the remains. If this is all their life represents, it is sad indeed. What about you? Will your life amount to more than a pile of junk at an estate sale?

Fill your lives with great thoughts, great people, and great deeds and you will live a rich life. There is a principle that restraint in one area of your life is a precursor to greater abundance in another, perhaps more meaningful area. Inner riches often come through outward simplicity.

Status seeking saps energy and steals time. Are you caught in a self-defeating cycle of pursuing vanity though social elevation? A friend who used to seek after worldly acclaim discovered, "It wasn't until I learned to let go that God started to bless my family. We are closer and more loving than ever before."

We all feel the desire at one time or another to be really free. Free to enjoy and appreciate. Free to express our inner selves. Free to soar to heights held only in the imagination. Free to love with no thought of self. Free to live with courage and strength. Free to hope. As you let go of whatever you are clutching and give your life to Jesus Christ, you will discover that freedom.

One woman told Kathy about a chance meeting she had the day before.

Yesterday I had to go to the hospital for some preliminary laboratory work. A young lady [sitting near me] doing cross-stitch shared that she was a manic depressive. "My husband left me, my mother left my father, I was beaten, and now I have to be on drugs the rest of my life." I told her, "I want you to remember this for the rest of your life. People—husbands and wives, children, neighbors, parents, and friends—will all disappoint you. There is one that will never let you down and that is Jesus Christ, and He will be there forever if you let Him."

"Pride goes before destruction, a haughty spirit before a fall" (Proverbs 16:18). Doubtlessly many men throughout history have been unknowingly playing out this three-thousand-year-old Jewish proverb. Charles was one of them.

Born in 1931 to lower-middle-class parents, Charles grew up in a waterfront suburb of Boston. His father was compelled to drop out of high school in order to support his mother and sister when his own father died. Charles's father worked days and attended night school. He married, continued night school, obtained an education in accounting and then law. It had taken twelve years. The influence of that dedicated work ethic had a tremendous influence on his son, Charles. So much so that some years later, President Nixon described him as a man who "would do anything" to achieve a goal.[6] Later Charles would also admit that "it was pride . . . that had propelled me through life."[7]

Charles graduated in 1949 from a small private school with honors and as valedictorian. He was voted most likely to succeed by his peers. His parents had sacrificed financially to send Charles to this particular school; it had been beyond their means and status. It was no doubt pride that later prompted Charles to turn down a full scholarship to Harvard because of its "condescension of aristocratic men to those who came out of less-fortunate backgrounds."[8] Instead, he accepted a full Navy ROTC scholarship at Brown University in Providence.

Never one to take the paved road, Charles always seemed to embrace the challenge of the difficult, the impossible. After graduation, he married, pursued a career, and attended law school in the evenings as his father had before him. Graduation from law school brought offers lesser men would have been honored to accept. Instead, he and a friend started their own law firm. Whether consciously or unconsciously, Charles was seeking the acceptance and respect of those who had spurned him in earlier years. The result was the same—an intense drive to succeed.

This preoccupation with business and politics put too much of a strain on his marriage. So after eleven years, it failed and ended in divorce. He refused to admit to himself that he had actually failed at something; his pride wouldn't let him. He remarried that same year. Politics became more a part of Charles's life. Leading a number of successful campaigns for politicians gave him the feeling that he indeed was a "kingmaker." There was no argument that he was good at what he did. So good in fact, that at age thirty-eight he became a member of the personal staff of the president of the United States.

Three years later, Charles W. Colson stood in deep reflection after having achieved his "fondest ambition"—being part of electing a president. But something wasn't right. "For three long years I had committed everything I had, every ounce of energy, to Richard Nixon's cause. Nothing else had mattered. We had had no time together as a family, no social life, no vacations. So why could my tongue not taste the flavor of this hour of conquest?"[9]

"What happened when there were no more mountains to scale? I was only forty-one. Surely there must be other stiff challenges. But what? What could I do next that would ever be as fulfilling as helping elect a President, being one of the small handful of men who each day made decisions that shaped the future of a nation?"[10] He thought about the pursuit of money. "But money—is that any real goal in life? No, the more I thought about it, the more one word seemed to sum up what was important to me. Pride."[11]

On June 3, 1974, Charles W. Colson pleaded guilty to one felony count of obstruction of justice. Sensitivity to the law had given way to expediency based on pride. On June 21, Charles was sentenced to one to three years in prison and fined $5,000. On July 8, he began to serve his sentence.

If the story ended there, all we have shown is that just one more person had gone astray, one more person had lived out the truth of the Jewish proverb. But the story doesn't end there. Sometime between November 1972 and June 1974, Charles W. Colson was guided to the point of realizing that he was not the master of his own destiny, that he needed God, and that he needed friends with whom he could honestly share his failures and feelings of inadequacy.[12]

Charles, as many before him, admits, "It was hard for me to grasp the enormity of this point—that Christ is the living God who promises us a day-to-day living relationship with Him and a personal one at that."[13] When Charles was given the opportunity to speak at his sentencing he said, "I have committed my life to Jesus Christ. I can work for the Lord in prison or out of prison, and that's how I want to spend my life."[14]

WHAT ABOUT YOU?

It is now fashionable to avoid conspicuous consumption. Are you jumping on the bandwagon just to be chic, or are you sincerely making changes so that you can more fully invest your life in that which is meaningful? Are you looking for that meaning in the concept of simplicity, or in the relationships that simplicity allows? The latter question is significant. One writer observes: "The problem is that contentment can't be found in the simple life, either. Maybe that's what Americans will spend the nineties searching for. They will be looking for contentment in the simple life because they couldn't find it in the 'good' life. . . . Contentment cannot be found without knowing the Shepherd. Jesus Christ is the door to contentment, and without Him you can't get there from here."[15]

E. M. Forster said, "I suggest that the only books that influence us are those for which we are ready, and which have gone a little farther down our particular path than we have yet got ourselves." We have traveled a long way on the road to a downscaled lifestyle and can attest to the rewards of those efforts, rewards that may not be tangible but are so much more meaningful; rewards that do not depend on monetary return but often come in the absence of excess; rewards that others look for in the riches of this world but that cannot even begin to be measured in dollars.

Downscaling is about relationships—meaningful, lasting relationships. But the only relationship that will ever satisfy completely is the one with Jesus Christ, the living God—the one who promises a living day-to-day personal relationship. And because of that relationship, all others will be much more meaningful.

James Dobson says:

I have concluded that the accumulation of wealth, even if I could achieve it, is an insufficient reason for living. When I reach the end of my days, a moment or two from now, I must look backward on something more meaningful than the pursuit of houses and land and machines and stocks and bonds. Nor is fame of any lasting benefit. I will consider my earthly existence to have been wasted unless I can recall a loving family, a consistent investment in the lives of people, and an earnest attempt to serve the God who made me. Nothing else makes much sense.[16]

NOTES

1. Stephanie Barlow, "Making It," *Entrepreneur* 20, no. 12 (December 1992), 103.

2. Ibid., 103.

3. "Letter of the Month," *Downscaling 46510,* August 1992, 6.

4. "Studies Find Youth Can't Tell Right from Wrong," *The Paper,* 9 September 1992, 16.

5. "Letter of the Month," *Downscaling 46510,* September 1992, 6.

6. "Colson Due to Surrender and Begins Sentence Today," *The New York Times,* July 8, 1974.

7. Charles W. Colson, *Born Again* (Old Tappan, New Jersey: Chosen, 1976), 114. All quotes from this work are used by permission.

8. Ibid., 24.

9. Ibid., 14.

10. Ibid., 21.

11. Ibid., 21.

12. Ibid., 11.

13. Ibid., 125.

14. Seymour M. Hersh, "Colson Reports Urging by Nixon: Gets 1–3 Years," *The New York Times,* 22 June 1974.

15. Steve Farrar, *If I'm Not Tarzan and My Wife Isn't Jane, What Are We Doing in the Jungle?* (Portland, Oreg.: Multnomah, 1991), 190.

16. James Dobson, *What Wives Wish Their Husbands Knew About Women* (Wheaton, Ill.: Tyndale, 1977), 108.

Selected Bibliography

Babbitt, Kathy J. *Habits of the Heart: Self-Discipline for the Not-So-Disciplined.* Brentwood, Tenn.: Wolgemuth & Hyatt, 1990.

Barna, George. *The Frog in the Kettle: What Christians Need to Know About Life in the Year 2000.* Ventura, Calif.: Regal, 1990.

Bradshaw, Charles, and Dave Gilbert. *Too Hurried to Love: Creating a Lifestyle for Lasting Relationships.* Eugene, Oreg.: Harvest, 1991.

Dayton, Howard, Jr. *Your Money: Frustration or Freedom.* Wheaton, Ill.: Tyndale, 1979.

DeGrote-Sorenson, Barbara, and David Allen Sorenson. *'Tis a Gift to Be Simple: Embracing the Freedom of Living with Less.* Minneapolis: Augsburg Fortress, 1992.

Elkind, David. *The Hurried Child: Growing Up Too Fast Too Soon.* Reading, Mass.: Addison-Wesley, 1981.

Family Research Council. *Free to Be Family.* Washington, D.C: 1992.

Farrar, Steve. *If I'm Not Tarzan and My Wife Isn't Jane, What Are We Doing in the Jungle?* Portland, Oreg.: Multnomah, 1991.

Golin, Mark, Mark Bricklin, and David Diamond. *Secrets of Executive Success.* Emmaus, Pa.: Rodale, 1991.

Hancock, Maxine. *Living on Less and Liking It More.* Chicago: Moody, 1976.

Harris, Greg. *The Home and Family Business Workshop.* Gresham, Oreg.: Christian Life Workshops, 1992.

Kimmel, Tim. *Surviving Life in the Fast Lane.* Colorado Springs: NavPress, 1990.

Kinder, Melvyn. *Going Nowhere Fast: Step Off Life's Treadmills and Find Peace of Mind.* New York: Fawcett Columbine, 1990, 80.

LaHaye, Tim. *How to Manage Pressure Before Pressure Manages You.* Grand Rapids: Zondervan, 1983.

Minear, Ralph E., and William Proctor. *Kids Who Have Too Much.* Nashville: Thomas Nelson, 1989.

Naisbitt, John, and Patricia Aburdene. *Megatrends Two Thousand: Ten New Directions for the 1990's.* New York: Avon, 1990.

O'Connor, Karen. *When Spending Takes the Place of Feeling.* Nashville: Thomas Nelson, 1992.

Peters, Thomas J., and Nancy K. Austin. *A Passion for Excellence: The Leadership Difference.* New York: Random, 1985.

Ross, Marilyn, and Tom Ross, *Country Bound!™ Trade Your Business Suit Blues for Blue Jean Dreams™*. Buena Vista, Colo.: Communication Creativity, 1992.

Saltzman, Amy. *Downshifting: Reinventing Success on a Slower Track.* New York: HarperCollins, 1991.

Sehnert, Keith W., M.D. *Stress/Unstress.* Minneapolis: Augsburg, 1981.

Sorenson, Stephen, and Amanda Sorenson. *Living Smart, Spending Less: Creative Ways to Stretch Your Income and Have Fun Doing It.* Chicago: Moody, 1993.

Welch, Bob. *More to Life Than Having It All: Living a Life You Won't Regret.* Eugene, Oreg. Harvest House, 1991.

For information on seminars and the availability of the newsletter *Downscaling 46510,* please write to:

Downscaling 46510
8782 S. Fisherman Cove
Claypool, IN 46510
(219) 566-2488

Subscriptions are $12.00 for 12 monthly issues. Back issues can be ordered 3 for $5.00, and a sample copy is $2.50.